Fit To Flourish

~

"Physical training is good, but training for godliness is much better, promising benefits in this life and in the life to come."

1 Timothy 4:8 (NLT)

A 31 day devotional journal encouraging personal study through the Psalms.

JANETTE KIEFFER

Redeeming Grace 99|1 Ministries
1001-A E. Harmony Rd.
#46
Fort Collins, Colorado 80525

TO JESUS; THE CHAMPION

Therefore, since we are surrounded by such a great cloud of witnesses, let us throw off everything that hinders and the sin that so easily entangles. And let us run with perseverance the race marked out for us, fixing our eyes on Jesus, the pioneer and perfecter of faith. For the joy set before him he endured the cross, scorning its shame, and sat down at the right hand of the throne of God. Consider him who endured such opposition from sinners, so that you will not grow weary and lose heart. Hebrews 12:1-3 (NIV)

~

…and to my parents, Mark and Mary Ellen, for "running" in such a way that spurs myself and others on; encouraging the passing of the baton of faith to the next generations at every opportunity.

As for me, I will always have hope; I will praise you more and more. My mouth will tell of your righteous deeds, of your saving acts all day long- though I know not how to relate them all. I will come and proclaim your mighty acts, Sovereign Lord; I will proclaim your righteous deeds, yours alone. Since my youth, God, you have taught me, and to this day I declare your marvelous deeds. Even when I am old and gray, do not forsake me, my God, till I declare your power to the next generation, your mighty acts to all who are to come. Your righteousness, God, reaches to the heavens, you who have done great things. Who is like you, God? Psalm 71:14-19 (NIV)

…and to my children, Noah, Maryelle, Faith, Micah, Elijah, Joshua, and my husband Christopher; who daily inspire me with their faith to keep on and "run" well this race God has set before us.

I love you for always, no matter what.
I will forever champion you.

I have no greater joy than to hear that my children are walking in the truth. 3 John 1:4 (NIV) For this reason I kneel before the Father, from whom every family in heaven and on earth derives its name. I pray that out of his glorious riches he may strengthen you with power through his Spirit in your inner being, so that Christ may dwell in your hearts through faith. And I pray that you, being rooted and established in love, may have power, together with all the Lord's holy people, to grasp how wide and long and high and deep is the love of Christ, and to know this love that surpasses knowledge— that you may be filled to the measure of all the fullness of God. Ephesians 3:14-19 (NIV)

CONTENTS

WELCOME FELLOW ATHLETE IN THE FAITH

Hi! I'm so very glad you have joined me on this journey to increase our spiritual fitness in Christ! Just as it is always easier to go with a friend to the gym for physical training, I hope as we spend the next 31 days in spiritual training together, you will consider me a friend as I do you - an answer to prayer kinda friend.

I believe it is no coincidence that you have come to this same page as I today. I have prayed for you and I, for all whom God would bring to open this book. My prayer is that we would each be given a greater understanding of His Book, the Bible, and a heart to apply it.

Let's commit to encourage one another to exercise daily in the pages of God's Word over the next month. (No need for spiritual flabbiness when God's "gym" is always open!) My prayer is that after a month of regularly saturating our souls with His Living Water and feasting on the Bread of Life (which is carb free by the way) healthy habits will form in our hearts and minds. I pray God stir a craving for more of Him in our lives, a craving only satisfied by ever increasing amounts of Him! By His grace may He continually make us fit to flourish in and through all things as we wholeheartedly abide in His presence.

ATHLETE'S ON YOUR MARK...

Do you not know that in a race all the runners run, but only one gets the prize? Run in such a way as to get the prize. Everyone who competes in the games goes into strict training. They do it to get a crown that will not last, but we do it to get a crown that will last forever. 1 Corinthians 9:24-25 (NIV)

I used to be on a cross country team. "Used to" being the operative words. When the water truck needs to come find you because you have gotten so far behind you've actually become lost, you begin to realize that maybe your competitive running career will be short lived.

I actually still enjoy running (The word "running" I use loosely. If you saw me you might call it a jog - if I'm lucky.) usually early in the morning as the sun is rising. It's time to clear my head, to worship, pray, listen to a podcast sermon… it often feels like all the world is still asleep except God and I and I get to watch Him slowly wake the world up with the sunrise. It's special. One thing a runner never forgets is that running requires endurance acquired through perseverance.

Watch your life and doctrine closely. Persevere in them… 1 Timothy 4:16 (NIV) For everything that was written in the past was written to teach us, so that through the endurance taught in the Scriptures and the encouragement they provide we might have hope. May the God who gives endurance and encouragement give you the same attitude of mind toward each other that Christ Jesus had, so that with one mind and one voice you may glorify the God and Father of our Lord Jesus Christ. Romans 15:4-6 (NIV)

Endurance is essential to success and is a gift of God however we are to maintain our endurance through offering ourselves to Him for His continuous filling. This can be a struggle because we live in a very loud and distracting world. A prayer of mine is that by His Spirits power I would always be captivated by Him, wholeheartedly enraptured by His unfailing love and that He would have my minds attention and hearts affection always. *For you have been given not only the privilege of trusting in Christ but also the privilege of suffering for him. We are in this struggle together. … Philippians 1:29-30 (NLT) But as for you, be strong and do not give up, for your work will be rewarded." 2 Chronicles 15:7 (NIV) …the one who endures to the end will be saved. Matthew 24:23 (ESV)*

Therefore, strengthen your feeble arms and weak knees. Hebrews 12:12 (NIV)
And by His amazing grace we will emerge from this study stronger; fit to flourish!

LET'S BEGIN!!!

~ DAY 1 ~

Date: _____

Hello my friend! Welcome to our spiritual gym! I'm so glad you met me here, thank you! **There is no better warm-up than worship so please name one thing you are grateful for.**

_____

_____

My brother once told me that before he get's out of bed, he wiggles his toes and his fingers and just says, "Thank you God." None of us are guaranteed to make it to the end of our moment let alone the end of the day, so let's thank Him for what we have, while we have it. Today I'm grateful He revived my soul and I woke up again because that means He has a purpose still to complete with my life today and God only purposes important things! If you are reading this He revived your soul this morning too and so your life too has divine purpose in this day! *I lie down and sleep; I wake again, because the LORD sustains me. Psalm 3:5 (NIV)* Oh dear one praise Him with me as we continue our worship in prayer.

Pray Scripture: *Let the morning bring me word of your unfailing love, for I have put my trust in you. Show me the way I should go, for to you I entrust my life. Psalm 143:8 (NIV)*

Please take time to open your personal time with the Lord in prayer.

Please record your prayer requests and or praise reports. This section of our time will be labeled: P.R. & P.R (prayer requests and praise reports). At the end of this 31 day journey you will have a record of the ways God has been working in your life through journaling your prayers and praises! ... *"My Father is always at his work to this very day, and I too am working." John 5:17 (NIV)*

In my kitchen our family has a whiteboard that we write down each family members prayer request for the week. (We usually do this on a Sunday at the lunch table after church.) This allows the family to be involved in the lives of one another in such a way that we can encourage each others spiritual endurance. If we see God answering or moving in those prayer requests throughout the week we add the praise report (in a different color) sharing in the joy of His faithfulness!

P.R. & P.R.

_____

_____

_____

_____

_____

_____

_____

_____

_____

_____

Daily Devotional Reading: "A Romance Like No Other"

We were made to flourish in any circumstance or situation. We were made to be a vessel of our God's victory! On our quest toward our eternal Home, we were made to thrive, not just survive dear one. When we choose to walk forward in faith, embracing the love displayed at the cross and living in the power of the resurrection, we "hope" through this broken world rather than just "cope" through it! Everlasting joy is found abiding in The Champion of Heaven!

By His divine power, God has given us everything we need for living a godly life. We have received all of this by coming to know him, the one who called us to himself by means of his marvelous glory and excellence. And because of his glory and excellence, he has given us great and precious promises. These are the promises that enable you to share his divine nature and escape the world's corruption caused by human desires. 2 Peter 1:3-4 (NLT)

Choosing to build our lives on the great and precious promises of our God, ensures an unshakable foundation upon which we will flourish through anything at any time! My prayer as we embark this month through His Word together is that we would embrace our true citizenship as children of God. Choosing to accept Jesus as your personal Savior affords you the free gift of His Holy Spirit changing your very heredity! It's not so much about changing human nature but rather cutting to the source of the sinfulness and imputing His divine nature, making us new as His divine children! *So if the Son sets you free, you will be free indeed.* John 8:36 (NIV)

Therefore, if anyone is in Christ, the new creation has come: The old has gone, the new is here! 2 Corinthians 5:17 (NIV) *For God so loved the world that he gave his one and only Son, that whoever believes in him shall not perish but have eternal life.* John 3:16 (NIV)

If you have never accepted Jesus as your personal Savior, I would encourage you to take time prayerfully in the verses below.

Romans 3:10 (NIV) As it is written: "There is no one righteous, not even one;

Romans 3:23 (NIV) for all have sinned and fall short of the glory of God,

Romans 6:23 (NIV) For the wages of sin is death, but the gift of God is eternal life in Christ Jesus our Lord.

Romans 5:8 (NIV) But God demonstrates his own love for us in this: While we were still sinners, Christ died for us.

Romans 10:9-10 (NIV) If you declare with your mouth, "Jesus is Lord," and believe in your heart that God raised him from the dead, you will be saved. For it is with your heart that you believe and are justified, and it is with your mouth that you profess your faith and are saved.

Romans 10:13 (NIV) for, "Everyone who calls on the name of the Lord will be saved."

Romans 5:1-2 (NIV) Therefore, since we have been justified through faith, we have peace with God through our Lord Jesus Christ, through whom we have gained access by faith into this grace in which we now stand. And we boast in the hope of the glory of God.

Romans 8:1 (NIV) Therefore, there is now no condemnation for those who are in Christ Jesus,

Maybe you feel ready to receive Him as your Savior if you have not already done so… there is no time like the present and there is no magic prayer to do so, just speak from your heart maybe something like this…

Dear Heavenly Father, I know I am a sinner in need of a Savior and I believe You, Jesus, are that Savior sent to die on the cross to pay the debt for my sin and offer forgiveness. I believe you rose again on the third day from the grave and live today. Thank you. Today, I give you my life Jesus. Amen.

Oh dear one, if you prayed that prayer today please know there is much rejoicing in Heaven! You can record the date below if you like as your spiritual birthday!

_____

I encourage you to find another believer whom you can share your decision for Christ with so that they can celebrate with you and help guide your spiritual growth.

2 Corinthians 1:20 (NIV) is one of my favorite Truth's and reminds us that, *For no matter how many promises God has made, they are "Yes" in Christ. And so through him the "Amen" is spoken by us to the glory of God.*

If we have been walking with the Lord for awhile the hope is that our lives would be speaking a confident "Yes!" to the promises of God as we navigate our sphere of influence. No matter how long our personal relationship with our God has been, are our lives displaying God confidence or are we exemplifying more of a shaky "I'm not so sure." in all that we face day to day?!

My prayer as we continue through His Word together this month is that in thought, word and action our lives would display a stark contrast to the way of the world as we rest, confident and secure as we grow in the precious and powerful promises of God. The world is searching for something to fill the dark void in it's heart and the only thing that satisfies that craving is Jesus Christ Himself, The Light of the World (John 8:12)!

LIGHT: L.ife I.n G.od H.olds T.ruth

Over the next 31 days let's commit to ingesting the Light of His Word that we might shine, reflecting Living Hope (1 Peter 1:3) in this world, to His praise and glory dear one! For He came to seek and save the lost (Luke 19:10)! He extends His heart to you in a nail scarred hand inviting you to experience a romance like no other, found only in Him, the very Creator of your soul.

Your word is a lamp to guide my feet and a light for my path. Psalm 119:105 (NLT)

Please proceed to our final portion of todays spiritual work out on the next page titled, "Study in the Psalms". Let's finish strong my friend, it will be well worth it!

Study in the Psalms:

There are 150 Psalms in the Bible. If we read 5 Psalms per day for the next 30 days allowing one additional day for Psalm 119 (the longest Psalm) we will have read through the entire book of Psalms in 31 days! So stick with me friend! Claim the promise tucked in Philippians 4:13 (NIV), *I can do all things through him who gives me strength.*

Today we will be reading Psalm 1, 2, 3, 4 and 5.

• Please read one Psalm at a time stopping to pray through anything that God brings to mind through His Word. Maybe you will stop to pray a verse out. Maybe you will stop and pray for help to live out a particular passage. Maybe you will pause and praise God for His faithfulness revealed to you in His Word. Just let God lead you though and take time to be still and listen to His voice as you lean in close to His heart.

• Before you move to reading the next Psalm in todays list, record the one verse that sticks out to you the most. (You will do these two bullet points for each Psalm on your list for each day.)

• My favorite verse from Psalm 1:

_____

_____

_____

• My favorite verse from Psalm 2:

_____

_____

_____

- My favorite verse from Psalm 3:

_____

_____

_____

- My favorite verse from Psalm 4:

_____

_____

_____

- My favorite verse from Psalm 5:

_____

_____

_____

- Now please read back through just the five verses that you recorded as having stood out to you the most. Do you feel like there is a similarity in the verses that stood out to you? Do you feel God whispering anything in particular to your individual heart through your reading with Him? *But Mary treasured up all these things and pondered them in her heart. Luke 2:19 (NIV)*

From where I sit, there are piles of snow outside my window. So I wish we each had a cup of coffee or tea (okay and maybe a few pieces of chocolate too) and could chat together over what God is revealing or challenging each of us with through the warmth of His Word. Maybe you have a friend, or family member closer than I that you could invite to gather with along this 31 day spiritual fitness challenge?!

Here are five simple points that stood out to me in the reading of Psalms 1-5 today. (These bullet points each day will make the most sense if you have already read the 5 assigned Psalms for the day.)

- Psalms 1-41 make up Book 1 of Psalms (there are 5 groupings total). The first two Psalms of this book 1 and the last two, Psalms 40-41 relay the theme of blessing upon those who make God's Word their delight and upon which they lay their trust.

- Psalm 1:1 shows a progression of walk, stand, sit… typically its a slow fade but a slippery slope when we start making allowances, loosening the boundaries God has set to give us the abundant life (see John 10:10). We may at first be only walking the sidelines of what we know is an activity or people group we should not be involved in or with only to find we are slowly coming to a stand and watch position (no longer walking by but hanging out around) until before we know it we are sitting at the table of wickedness and fully participating our selves. (See 1 Peter 5:8, 2 Corinthians 11:14, 1 Corinthians 10:13 for further study.)

- Psalm 2:2-3 alludes to the breaking of chains, humans thinking they are in control and can do what they like. Yes, God died to give us free will but who cuts the break lines in their car so that they can drive unhindered!? I like that illustration given to me, as it paints such a clear picture of how silly and dangerous it is when I choose not to adhere to God's Word; His best way (see John 10:10 again)! Don't cut your ties to your Creator dear one, He IS God, He died to give you the best and eternal life, honor Him with obedience to the boundaries He has set in His Word for your absolute freedom.

- Psalm 2:4 reflects Acts 4:25. (See Acts 4:23-31 for further study.) Nothing is out of our Almighty Sovereign God's good hand dear one, no matter what it feels like or appears to be. If we will lay our trust on His Word by His Spirit and pray as the believers did in Acts 4:29 (NIV) *Now, Lord, consider their threats and enable your servants to speak your word with great boldness.* How differently would our lives reflect our God, exuding a strength and peace in and through any circumstance?! Acts 4:31 (NIV) reports, *After they prayed, the place where they were meeting was shaken. And they were all filled with the Holy Spirit and spoke the word of God boldly.* Sounds like they were made - fit to flourish!

- Psalm 4:8 and Psalm 3:5, am to pm God is with me, with you, so we can rest and rise in peace dear one. Between the resting and the rising or the sleep hours and the wakeful hours of life there can be the waiting hours. When we wait in God we can wait with expectancy as Psalm 5:3 indicates. *Let us hold unswervingly to the hope we profess, for he who promised is faithful. Hebrews 5:13 (NIV)* Living in expectancy of His faithfulness frees us from our own boxed in expectations of how we think our life should go. *...Blessed are all who wait for him! Isaiah 30:18 (NIV) Now to him who is able to do immeasurably more than all we ask or imagine, according to his power that is at work within us, Ephesians 3:20 (NIV) However, as it is written: "What no eye has*

seen, what no ear has heard, and what no human mind has conceived"
— the things God has prepared for those who love him— 2 Corinthians
2:9 (NIV)

- Please record what you feel is God's specific Word to you today.
  We could call this part our "cool down" (what typically happens at
  the end of a good work out). Our "cool down" is where we record
  what will help us keep our cool all through the day. His Word to us
  that we can tuck in our hearts so that our lives speak a confident
  "yes and amen!" to His faithful promises. Record what you have
  mined in His Word that has equipped you to confidently declare in
  Him, "I am fit to flourish!"

_____

_____

_____

_____

_____

_____

_____

Thank you for joining me in God's "gym" today dear one, You have
been a spiritual encouragement to me. See you back here tomorrow!

God bless you muchly~

~ DAY 2 ~

Date: _____

You came back!! Welcome dear one, beloved of God! I'm so grateful you are here! I don't know about you, but personally, I'm glad I don't need to put on a swim suit to dive into the water of God's Word today! My cozy slippers and pullover sweatshirt will do just fine!

Warm Up with Worship:
Please record one thing you are grateful for today.

_____

_____

Psalm 3:6 (NIV) I will not fear though tens of thousands assail me on every side. I'm grateful that I can chose not to fear no matter what assails me in my mind, on my agenda, through the diagnosis… as overwhelming as "it" can threaten to be, my God is the God of Deuteronomy 20:4 (NIV) that states, *For the Lord your God is the one who goes with you to fight for you against your enemies to give you victory."* And 2 Timothy 4:18 (NIV) *The Lord will rescue me from every evil attack and will bring me safely to his heavenly kingdom. To him be glory for ever and ever. Amen.*

Pray Scripture: *They were all trying to frighten us, thinking, "Their hands will get too weak for the work, and it will not be completed." But I prayed, "Now strengthen my hands." Nehemiah 6:9 (NIV)* Dear Heavenly Father strengthen our hands that our lives would bear fruit to your glory today. … Maybe you can further personalize Nehemiah 6:9 to your own life situations and circumstances. Let this time lead you into your opening personal prayer time with the God of Heavens Armies.

P.R. & P.R. (Prayer Requests and Praise Reports)

_____

_____

_____

_____

_____

_____

_____

_____

_____

_____

Daily Devotional Reading: "Fit To Flourish"

The righteous will flourish like a palm tree, they will grow like a cedar of Lebanon; planted in the house of the Lord, they will flourish in the courts of our God. They will still bear fruit in old age, they will stay fresh and green, proclaiming, "The Lord is upright; he is my Rock, and there is no wickedness in him." Psalm 92:12-15 (NIV)

Hmmm fit to... flourish like a palm tree...planted in the house of the Lord... flourishing in His courts...bearing fruit in old age (can I get an amen on that flourishing fresh in old age bit?!!)... This whole palm tree thing got me digging further. What I found proves to be more effective than any anti aging cream or self help book out there!

Side note: I moved to Arizona from Wisconsin as a kid and one thing I remember that thrilled me was the sight of palm trees! Palm trees in my Wisconsin winter grown mind symbolized paradise! The place people went for sun soaked vacations! I have since moved back to a land of four seasons and enjoy the creativity of our God in the passionately painted red leaves of maples! So I guess my point is that no matter where you reside geographically, paradise is found in the presence of our God alone.

Okay, back to my research on the palm trees in Scripture. A glance at temple construction finds carvings of palm trees in liberal amounts!

On the walls all around the temple, in both the inner and outer rooms, he carved cherubim, palm trees and open flowers. 1 Kings 6:29 (NIV)

In the space above the outside of the entrance to the inner sanctuary and on the walls at regular intervals all around the inner and outer sanctuary were carved cherubim and palm trees. Palm trees alternated with cherubim…. From the floor to the area above the entrance, cherubim and palm trees were carved on the wall of the main hall. Ezekiel 41:17-18, 20 (NIV)

If we choose to root down and dwell in the shelter of the Most High we will be a planting, a display of His splendor (Psalm 91:1, Isaiah 61:3)! Fruitfulness or our effectiveness for His Kingdom is guaranteed as we remain in Him (John 15:4-5)! As palms extend upward moved by the wind so should we be! By this I mean we can choose to allow God to be the lifter of our heads, choose to seek His face and strength continually as our sustaining Source of life (Psalm 3:3, 105:4, John 6:35)!

If it were his intention and he withdrew his spirit and breath, all humanity would perish together and mankind would return to the dust. "If you have understanding, hear this; listen to what I say. Job 34:14-16 (NIV)

Dear one, *He is before all things, and in him all things hold together.* Colossians 1:17 (NIV) so why so often do we go off chasing "things" when all "things" need to be held together?! Just pursue The Heart that holds all things together and is ever pursuing yours; experience the greatest romance of all time!

Ephesians 3:19 (ESV) invites us to experience the fullness of God! *And to know the love of Christ that surpasses knowledge, that you may be filled with all the fullness of God.*

It is the breath or Spirit of God that sustains all life. As the palm leaves move with the wind we too want to be moved by His Spirit.

John 3:8 (NLT) *The wind blows wherever it wants. Just as you can hear the wind but can't tell where it comes from or where it is going, so you can't explain how people are born of the Spirit."*

We have a God bigger than we can comprehend and praise that we do! He is infinite, infinite love, grace, mercy, justice… He is always all of Himself. When He moves it is with total infinite wisdom on all levels! With my finite mind I have no capacity to comprehend it all but that leaves room for ever increasing amounts of trust and we can trust, for He who promised is faithful (Hebrews 10:23)!

John 20:22 (NIV) *And with that he breathed on them and said, "Receive the Holy Spirit.*

Acts 2:2,4 (NIV) *Suddenly a sound like the blowing of a violent wind came from heaven and filled the whole house where they were sitting....All of them were filled with the Holy Spirit...*

Ezekiel 37:9-14 (NIV) *Then he said to me, "Prophesy to the breath; prophesy, son of man, and say to it, 'This is what the Sovereign Lord says: Come, breath, from the four winds and breathe into these slain, that they may live.'" So I prophesied as he commanded me, and breath entered them; they came to life and stood up on their feet—a vast army. Then he said to me: "Son of man, these bones are the people of Israel. They say, 'Our bones are dried up and our hope is gone; we are cut off.' Therefore prophesy and say to them: 'This is what the Sovereign Lord says: My people, I am going to open your graves and bring you up from them; I will bring you back to the land of Israel. Then you, my people, will know that I am the Lord, when I open your graves and bring you up from them. I will put my Spirit in you and you will live, and I will settle you in your own land. Then you will know that I the Lord have spoken, and I have done it, declares the Lord.'"*

Philippians 2 reminds us Jesus emptied Himself when He came to be born on earth. He emptied Himself, not of His divinity but of His divine powers. He did all He did here by the power of the Holy Spirit as He walked obedient to the Father's will. When Jesus ascended back to heaven after His death and resurrection He promised to send the gift of His Spirit, that same Spirit that raised Him from the grave to come live with us as believers!!

Romans 8:11 (NLT) *The Spirit of God, who raised Jesus from the dead, lives in you. And just as God raised Christ Jesus from the dead, he will give life to your mortal bodies by this same Spirit living within you.*

As we immerse ourselves in the water of His Word this month may we flourish like palm trees in His presence, bearing fruit even into our old age, moved by the wind of the Spirit and always lifting His name high as a display of His splendor!

Dear one, you were made to be completely fit to flourish!! *Do you not know that in a race all the runners run, but only one gets the prize? Run in such a way as to get the prize. Everyone who competes in the games goes into strict training. They do it to get a crown that will not last, but we do it to get a crown that will last forever.* 1 Corinthians 9:24-25 (NIV)

Are you ready to dive deeply into His Word?! As we follow Christ's lead, by His grace may we leave a path of faith for those yet to come. *Follow my example, as I follow the example of Christ.* 1 Corinthians 11:1 (NIV) May He write His Word on the tablets of our hearts. *Let this be written for a future generation, that a people not yet created may praise the LORD:* Psalm 102:18 (NIV)

Please bow in prayer to honor His leadership once more and to ask that He stir His Spirit within us, that we might understand beyond what we could ever comprehend on our own, that He would teach us great and unsearchable things we do not know and we would grow fit to flourish, as a display of His splendor as He always intended dear one (Job 32:8, Jeremiah 33:3).

Study in the Psalms: Today we will be reading through Psalm 6, 7, 8, 9 and 10.

Remember to converse with God as you read through each Psalm. Pause and reflect on verses that catch your heart's attention. Record one verse from each Psalm below that particularly holds impact for you and review your list. Is there a theme in the verses you highlighted? Take time and listen for God's voice to your heart.

- My favorite verse from Psalm 6:

_____

_____

- My favorite verse from Psalm 7:

_____

_____

- My favorite verse from Psalm 8:

_____

_____

- My favorite verse from Psalm 9:

_____

_____

_____

• My favorite verse from Psalm 10:

_____

_____

_____

As you ponder over God's Word to you in your heart, here are five simple points that stood out to me in our reading today. (Remember, these bullet points each day will make the most sense if you have already read the 5 assigned Psalms for the day.)

• Psalm 6:1 parallels Jeremiah 10:24 for me in that Jeremiah along with David are well aware that under justice without mercy NONE of us could stand. Praise our God who is 100% just AND 100% mercy, 100% of the time! We spoke of swim suit attire at the beginning of our day… it seems in Psalm 6:6 David has found himself swimming in his own tears. God welcomes our open honesty and in that He can shift our focus from self to Himself. We have a God full of grace, unfailing love, forgiveness and gentle mercy. _Come to me, all you who are weary and burdened, and I will give you rest. Take my yoke upon you and learn from me, for I am gentle and humble in heart, and you will find rest for your souls. Matthew 11:28-29 (NIV) Let us then approach God's throne of grace with confidence, so that we may receive mercy and find grace to help us in our time of need. Hebrews 4:16 (NIV)_

• Psalm 7:8 reveals David's total reliance upon sustained truth. Notice that the first letter of each word in that phrase: total reliance upon sustained truth, spells the word TRUST. Considering

David's sin (see 2 Samuel 11) he was still able to confidently declare his innocence! Yet this is the kind of pure conscience and bold confidence that comes from trusting totally in God's faithful Word! When God forgives it is total and it is His righteousness that clothes us completely! *If we confess our sins, he is faithful and just and will forgive us our sins and purify us from all unrighteousness. 1 John 1:9 (NIV) I delight greatly in the LORD; my soul rejoices in my God. For he has clothed me with garments of salvation and arrayed me in a robe of righteousness, as a bridegroom adorns his head like a priest, and as a bride adorns herself with her jewels. Isaiah 61:10 (NIV)*

- Our minds are finite and our God is infinite. We have no way of comprehending His ways. (See Isaiah 55:8-9) However when we submit in humility to our Creator and trust His proven faithfulness we soar rather than becoming sore and sour. *But those who hope in the LORD will renew their strength. They will soar on wings like eagles; they will run and not grow weary, they will walk and not be faint. Isaiah 40:31 (NIV)* Psalm 8:4 in the NKJV uses the word "visit". Who are we that God would visit us?! And yet He did, as a baby, Immanuel which means God with us (Matthew 1:23) and He continues to be with us! When you contemplate the word, visit, you think of who you might visit… a sickly neighbor, a prisoner, someone who lives alone… why?!; to communicate your loving care. Jesus came to visit earth to reveal His everlasting love and presence with us. *Beyond all question, the mystery from which true godliness springs is great: He appeared in the flesh, was vindicated by the Spirit, was seen by angels, was preached among the nations, was believed on in the world, was taken up in glory. 1 Timothy 3:16 (NIV) just as the Son of Man did not come to be served, but to serve, and to give his life as a random for many." Matthew 20:28 (NIV) ... surely I am with you always, to the very end of the age." Matthew 28:20 (NIV)* You are loved and in all you may not understand this side of heaven you are not asked to walk it out alone. *For now we see only a reflection as in a mirror; then we shall see face to face. Now I know in part; then I shall know fully, even as I am fully known. 1 Corinthians 13:12 (NIV)*

- In reading through the Psalms, always look for an attribute of God or a characteristic of His that you can praise Him for. It's easy to read Scripture looking for how to find help for ourselves, and we should, the more we look for Him, know Him, the more we actually help ourselves! How often can we say we WHOLE heartedly praise Him as Psalm 9:1 indicates praise coming from a whole heart? How might choosing to praise Him wholeheartedly for who He is, change our attitude toward what we face? *That is why I am suffering as I am. Yet this is no cause for shame, because I know whom I have believed, and am convinced that he is able to guard what I have entrusted to him until that day. 2 Timothy 1:12 (NIV)* "But blessed is the one who trusts in the Lord, whose confidence is in him. Jeremiah 17:7 (NIV)

- Psalm 10:15 is a prayer to turn inward. (NIV) *Break the arm of the wicked man; call the evildoer to account for his wickedness that would not otherwise be found out.* Dear God, break the wicked in me, search even the unconscious parts of me, check my motives and intentions and purify me... Psalm 139:23-24 (NIV) is a good passage to turn into prayer for help in this area too, *Search me, God, and know my heart, test me and know my anxious thoughts. See if there is any offensive way in me, and lead me in the way everlasting.* He will faithfully lead, in His strength, by His grace may He grant me a willing spirit to follow in faithful obedience.

Here is the part of our spiritual fitness routine we like to call our "cool down". Record the coolest thing God gifted you today through your time in His Word.

_____

_____

_____

_____

_____

_____

_____

Thank you for your time today my flourishing fit sister in the faith! God bless you muchly~

~ DAY 3 ~

Date: _____

Welcome! Day three and still going strong, I sure appreciate you showing up. This morning I was looking out across my snow covered backyard with multiple freshly filled bird feeders and yet still no birds! As I worried about all my feathered friends not knowing where to find food in the snow I was reminded that God reminds us not to worry, not even about the birds! *Look at the birds of the air; they do not sow or reap or store away in barns,* (So that must mean it all falls on my shoulders to provide for these little ones!!! Not so much... I must keep reading.) *and yet your heavenly Father feeds them.* (Oooh! It's on His shoulders not mine. He may provide for them through me but if they are not coming to my feeders I must trust that they are being provided for elsewhere. He says He feeds them and so He does and He is, for no word from God ever fails (Luke 1:37). *Are you not much more valuable than they? Can any one of you by worrying add a single hour to your life? Matthew 6:26-27 (NIV)* I can't even make the birds come so adding hours to my life is out of the question! But wouldn't you know, just as I sat down to write, a Blue Jay showed up!! Just one, but one was all I needed to remind me that He sees, He cares, He is moving.

When we don't feel like we can see His hand or hear His voice I have been reminded to trust His heart which is always revealed in His faithful Word. You, dear one, and all that weighs on your heart, matters to God. If He is faithfully providing for the birds (and He is) then you can count on Him sustaining you even in what may seem like a winter season. *Then Jesus told him, "Because you have seen me, you have believed; blessed are those who have not seen and yet have believed." John 20:29 (NIV) But when you ask him, be sure that your faith is in God alone. Do not waver, for a person with divided loyalty is as unsettled as a wave of the sea that is blown and tossed by the wind. James 1:6 (NLT)* "be sure that your faith is in God alone." There are many waves in this world that would like to wash us up on having placed our faith in things rather that in the One who holds all "things" together (Colossians 1:17).

Warm Up with Worship: (Phew! After that long winded beginning I hope you're not actually worn out!) Please record one thing you are thankful for today.

_____

_____

Like I said, I'm grateful YOU showed up today!

Pray Scripture: *This is the day that the LORD has made; let us rejoice and be glad in it. Psalm 118:24 (ESV)* Dear Heavenly Father, THIS IS the day that You have created and without a doubt the breath in my lungs and the beat in my heart is Your gift to me for such a time as this! I choose to rejoice and be glad in this present moment trusting that what You purpose, You provide for. Thank You for Your Word, for when I think on Truth I have no room for my worries. *You will keep in perfect peace those whose minds are steadfast, because they trust in you. Isaiah 26:3 (NIV)* Thank You, in Jesus name…

Please take a moment to continue to open your personal time in the Word with God in prayer.

P.R. & P.R.

_____

_____

_____

_____

_____

_____

_____

_____

_____

_____

Daily Devotional Reading: "Happy New Year?!?"

At the time I am writing this it is January so the "Happy New Year" theme works for my present time. However I understand it may be the middle of July for you… and yet each new day is really the beginning of a brand new year, right?! So no matter what time of year you are reading this I pray you will find it impactful.

"Happy New Year!" is the nationally accepted exclamation spoken over 365 days of the… unknown!!?! How many other situations or circumstances in your life have held that much unknown and you decided to take that same worry free, happy mindset? The world as a whole has somehow decided on the first day of the year to embrace the unknown… filled with HOPE! So then what happens in the unknown of our moments throughout the rest of our days that changes that mindset so often to worry?

The only way a person can maintain a mindset of sure hope in a world of unknowns is to anchor it to the Living Word of God (Hebrews 6:19). Life in this broken world has always guaranteed troubles (John 16:33).

- Every David has a Shimei throwing the dirt of past failures in your face (2 Sam. 16:5-13)
- Every Naomi has an Orpah that leaves instead of remaining loyal (Ruth)
- Every Sampson has a Delilah sized temptation struggle (Judges 16)
- Every Jonah has a Ninavah - a job that just grinds (Jonah)
- Every Job has comforters that are just making things worse (Job)
- Every Hannah has a Peninnah who in jealousy kicks you when you're down (1 Sam. 1-2)
- Every Esther has an evil Haman trying to kill God's plan for your life (Esther)

So how do we overcome without being overcome?!

We do this by keeping our eyes on Jesus, the champion who initiates and perfects our faith. Because of the joy awaiting him, he endured the cross, disregarding its shame. Now he is seated in the place of honor besides God's throne. Think of all the hostility he endured from sinful people; then you won't become weary and give up. Hebrews 12:2-3 (NLT)

Each individual listed above proved faithful in the end drawing on the faithfulness of God; our God. *But you, Lord, are a shield around me, my glory, the One who lifts my head high. Psalm 3:3 (NIV)* 365 days a year we can feast on the Bread of Life, the very Word of God which will faithfully sustain us in every moment.

Every new year can be welcomed with the authentic exclamation of "Happy New Year!" for those in Jesus, because happy is each year that brings us nearer to His sure return! *He will wipe every tear from their eyes. There will be no more death' or mourning or crying or pain, for the old order of things has passed away." He who was seated on the throne said, "I am making everything new!" Then he said, "Write this down, for these words are trustworthy and true." Revelation 21:4-5 (NIV)*

In the ups and downs of the unknown this year, remember dear one, beloved of God, …*despite all these things, overwhelming victory is ours through Christ, who loved us. Romans 8:37 (NLT)*

Study in the Psalms: Today we will be reading through Psalms 11, 12, 13, 14 and 15.

- Converse with God as you read through each Psalm.
- Pause and reflect on verses that catch your heart's attention.
- Record one verse from each Psalm that holds impact for you.
- Review your list. Is there a theme in the verses you highlighted? Take time and listen for God's voice to your heart.

- My favorite verse from Psalm 11:

_____

_____

_____

- My favorite verse from Psalm 12:

_____

_____

_____

- My favorite verse from Psalm 13:

_____

_____

_____

- My favorite verse from Psalm 14:

_____

_____

_____

- My favorite verse from Psalm 15:

  _____

  _____

  _____

As you ponder over God's Word to you in your heart, here are five simple points that stood out to me in our reading today. (I won't continue to remind, but the bullet points each day will make more sense if the daily assigned reading in the Psalms is first completed.)

- I appreciate David's response to the advise given to him to run away from his troubles in Psalm 11:1. He wonders why in the world would someone suggest that he be fearful when his refuge, his trust was in God Almighty!! But look… the enemy is aiming for you and the the foundations are being destroyed and even the shadows are not safe… what about the lab results or your diagnosis, or your financial standing or your failing relationships or that job loss?! Don't you think you should run and worry and be very afraid?!! Dear one, do not give in to the temptation to let the enemies tactics tear away the Truth you hold!! Like David in this Psalm 11 we must confidently place our trust and hope in our God Who is on His throne even still (verse 4) and even when the wrong seems strong He is the Ruler and His reign will never end and His children will not be overcome but will make it safely to His Heavenly Kingdom for all eternity (2 Timothy 4:18)!!!

- Time never stops. Sometimes it may seem we are always running!

We will always run in the direction of our focus. Let our focus be on Jesus and His faithful Word (see Hebrews 12:1-3). Psalm 12:6 declares God's Word to be flawless! Flawless!! It's not the words but rather the One who spoke the words that gives them their flawless power. Any one can say, let their be light, and yet the room will remain just as dark as before. However when darkness hovered over the deep in the beginning of creation back in Genesis, it was because God, the Author of all authority said, *"Let their be light,"* (Genesis 1:3) that our world lit up!! So who's word do you allow to hold power in your life? Dear one, may it only ever be the flawless Word of God Almighty that holds the loudest volume and the greatest impact in your heart. Navigate life from; let your life's validation be; only that of God Almighty.

- Four times in the first two verses of Psalm 13 the "how long?!" question is asked! Does this sound like anyone else's road trips too?! Life can be a real trip, like a road trip! Yet in just 6 total verses that David spent pondering with God he was given proper perspective! Prayer does change things but sometimes the most powerful change that occurs is within the individual doing the praying. Pondering our problems in prayer with God can allow Him the time He needs to point us to the point of our questions. A question mark always has a dot, or a point at the bottom of that squiggly mark right?!? We all want the quick exclamation mark life. Excited, joyful and the point of our journey is clearly seen from the top! However our perseverance grows in the trials and perseverance produces maturity to the point we do not lack anything, James 1:1-4 reminds us. So we can choose joy in our trials, in our questions if we, like David did, take our problems and ponder them with God for as long as it takes, persevering until our perspective is framed to His perfect way.

- Psalm 14:1 reminds us there is no one good which reflects the Truth of *Romans 3:12 (NIV) All have turned away, they have together become worthless; there is no one who does good, not even one."* No one, includes you and I. By God's grace He moved first! While we were still sinners He died for us (Romans 5:8) our faith, our salvation is a free gift because it cost Him everything! No sin is less than another when every sin cost the cross. Might this Psalm stir in us a humility to allow or even invite others to come play, or do life on the same playing field of grace as we are?! After all, it's the only playing field ANY of us could stand on because of His amazing grace! *He has shown you, O mortal, what is good. And what does the Lord require of you? To act justly and to love mercy and to walk humbly with your God. Micah 6:8 (NIV)*

- Psalm 15:4 talks about keeping promises even when it hurts. In a world where broken promises are a norm, this verse holds up a stark contrast found in Jesus. His love is unending, His Word unfailing and through His Spirit we can endure in keeping our promises even when it hurts. Those who take up life in Jesus, living out the Word and not just hearing it (even when it's hard) will not be shaken just as verse 5 indicates! There will be times our mood does not match our mission and we feel shaky however feelings are not facts and God's Word never fails. When we choose to live trusting and obeying His Word, … *"Love the Lord your God with all your heart and with all your soul and with all your mind.' … 'Love your neighbor as yourself.' Matthew 22:37-39 (NIV)* Our lives reflect Jesus. Loving others is standing with our arms outstretched and loving God is us loving upward… does this not paint a picture of the cross with or lives! *John 12:32 (NIV) And I, when I am lifted up from the earth, will draw all people to myself."* When we allow the life of Jesus to be lifted high on our lives, when we live sacrificially and submitted to His best way, His Kingdom is furthered! John 12:32 reminds us He can do a work far greater in and through our lives than we could ever, ever do on our own, but we need to get down and out of the way so that He can be in His rightful place, high and lifted up! *For whoever wants to save their life will lose it, but whoever loses their life for me will save it. Luke 9:24 (NIV)*

"Cool Down": Record the coolest thing or the point that God gifted you today through your time in His Word that will help you keep your cool.

_____

_____

_____

_____

_____

_____

_____

Thank you for meeting me here on this page and within His powerful Word today! God bless you muchly~ *Now may the God of peace, who through the blood of the eternal covenant brought back from the dead our Lord Jesus, that great Shepherd of the sheep, equip you with everything good for doing his will, and may he work in us what is please to him, through Jesus Christ, to whom be glory for ever and ever. Amen. Hebrews 13:20-21 (NIV)*

~ DAY 4 ~

Date: _____

Hello my friend! I hope you are beginning to feel the groove and comfort of a routine forming. Or spiritual strength and stamina will increase as we regularly receive His Word. I do say, "receive", because a gift is only experienced fully if it is unwrapped and actually received. In James 1:5 we are reminded that God will give His wisdom generously to all who would ask for it. However how often to we really want it? How often do we ask for His wisdom and yet feel tossed on the waves of doubt as James 1:6 indicates is possible? Could it be that we are not really ready to receive God's wisdom because we are double-minded (James 1:8), waffling, really undecided between wanting our own wisdom and God's? What would it mean to really receive God's wisdom? I know in my life it means accepting His way even when, even if, even though... it means in humility, in holy fear, submitting to His best way in all of life. In thought, word and action in all areas of my life allowing God's way to rule and reign first, over and above my own. This can only be done in the Spirits power but I first have to be willing to submit to His filling. *1 Thessalonians 5:19 (NIV) Do not quench the Spirit.* Wise advice. Jesus died to give us free choice. Our best life will be not only in acknowledging God as God but also as allowing Him to be Lord of our lives.

Warm Up and Worship:

He is worthy of all our worship, please record one thing you are grateful for today.

_____

_____

Pray Scripture: *May these words of my mouth and this meditation of my heart be pleasing in your sight, Lord, my Rock and my Redeemer. Psalm 19:14 (NIV)* Dear Heavenly Father, we desire to give You our wholehearted attention and hearts affection. Help us to honor Your leadership through our obedient following. … Please continue to open your time with God today in prayer.

P.R. & P.R. (Prayer Requests & Praise Reports)

I have one! If you were with me yesterday you might remember I had written about the one little Blue Jay visitor at my backyard feeder. Today I praise God that I had FIVE Blue Jays and sparrows! *From his abundance we have all received one gracious blessing after another. John 1:16 (NLT)*

_____

_____

_____

_____

_____

_____

_____

Daily Devotional Reading: "Enjoy The Journey" Based on
Psalm 13 which we studied yesterday!

*How long, LORD? Will you forget me forever? How long will you hide your
face from me? Psalm 13:1 (NIV)*

Remember taking vacations as a kid and how you NEVER got tired
of asking, "Are we there yet?!" Now that we are older we just check
our gps map incessantly to receive affirmation that we are on the
right route and making forward progress toward our destination. No
matter how insignificantly the little blue dot (that represents us)
seems to be moving, the fact that it is on the map and on the
recorded route, gives us hope and we confidently declare to anyone
asking, "Are we there yet?!" within our caravan...

"Don't worry, we will make it, just enjoy the ride!" (See Phil. 4:13)

This reminds me of Psalm 13. In just the first 2 verses David has
asked God FOUR times how much longer?! David feels forgotten,
ignored, filled with sorrow and exhausted from wrestling with the
unknown; He wonders how long will it be that the enemy seems to
have the upper hand in triumph over him?! I'm sure any human can
relate to some sort of "How long...?!" of their own. Here in Psalm
13 we find refreshing hope for our "How longs?"!!

Psalm 13:3 reveals David's level of distress that if God doesn't bring him some Light he may just die! Yet in all of his feelings of running out of everything it takes to go on, he runs to the only One all things run on (Acts 17:28, Col. 1:16-17, John 1:3) and God is faithful. (John 1:5)

David's sigh is turned to song, as he pulled away to pray and release everything he had left into the hands of his Heavenly Father, he found relief! His mind was renewed and his heart refreshed, NOT because his wait was over but because, ...*those who wait on the LORD shall renew their strength; They shall mount up with wings like eagles, They shall run and not be weary, They shall walk and not faint. Isaiah 40:31 (NKJV)* Have you ever seen how high an eagle can fly?! It soars at heights that appear impossible! (Matthew 19:26) In our God we have resurrection strength that exceeds our feelings and if we are willing to choose it, we too can rise above our situation and circumstance.

We have sustaining strength available that rises up even when the waiting threatens to weigh us down. We find it when… our hearts' affection and minds' attention are enraptured, totally captivated by God's faithfulness, His unfailing love, kindness and trustworthy promises, found through time spent with Him in His Word and in prayer.

Are we there yet?! No, not yet dear one, but by my map (His faithful and unfailing Word that endures forever (1 Peter 1:25)) ...*it is written: "What no eye has seen, what no ear has heard, and what no human mind has conceived"* - *the things God has prepared for those who love him- 1 Corinthians*

2:9 (NIV) Oh praise the One who is our Way in the wait!!! (John 14:1-6)

Don't worry, in Jesus we will make it, so just enjoy the journey! (2 Tim. 4:18, 2 Cor. 2:14)

Study in the Psalms: Today we will be reading Psalms 16, 17, 18, 19 and 20. I can't wait to enjoy this journey with you!

- Converse with God as you read through each Psalm.
- Pause and reflect on verses that catch your heart's attention.
- Record one verse from each Psalm that holds impact for you.
- Review your list. Is there a theme in the verses you highlighted? Take time and listen for God's voice to your heart.

- My favorite verse from Psalm 16:

_____

_____

_____

- My favorite verse from Psalm 17:

_____

_____

_____

- My favorite verse from Psalm 18:

_____

_____

_____

- My favorite verse from Psalm 19:

_____

_____

_____

- My favorite verse from Psalm 20:

_____

_____

_____

As you ponder over the treasures God has tucked into your heart here are five points I found intriguing through our reading today.

- *Psalm 16:2 (NLT) I said to the LORD, "You are my Master!…* Notice the psalmist, David is acknowledging God as God but also Master of his own life. How often do I forfeit my own peace and joy because although I'm asking for God's way I'm really wrestling with wanting my own? I'm wrestling not resting. Psalm 16:7 finds David declaring he would bless the Lord who guides him. Do we bless or begrudge God's guidance in our lives? The rest of the Psalm declares the joy and peace experienced when we are willing to let God Almighty lead. Our joy and peace is not found in our circumstance but rather in resting in His faithful presence. We are never alone, He will never fail us nor forsake us and He will bring us through to the safety of His Heavenly Kingdom (see Matthew 28:20, Hebrews 13:5, 2 Timothy 4:18). Keep His gift of faith and do not give up for He who promised is faithful (see Hebrews 10:23).

- Psalm 17:8 references being guarded or kept as God's eye. I've heard that the fastest reflex in the body is the blink of an eye to protect itself. God, our Creator of that reflexive speed is able to move even faster then the blink of an eye in our defense! Psalm 17:4 tells us David was kept from wrong doing by way of God's Word. Just as Jesus was able to withstand the devil's tricks in the desert by knowing Truth so well (see Matthew 4). His Word will also be our greatest weapon against the enemies schemes! *For the word of God is alive and active. Sharper than any double-edged sword, it penetrates even to dividing soul and spirit, joints and marrow; it judges the thoughts and attitudes of the heart. Hebrews 4:12 (NIV)* In the Psalms we see the focus and attention is on God. When we spend regular daily time in the Word our focus is much more likely to default to His Truth in our trials rather than trip on then enemies traps. *Be alert and of sober mind. Your enemy the devil prowls around like a roaring lion looking for someone to devour. 1 Peter 5:8 (NIV)*

- I'm not sure if you were able to pick just one verse from Psalm 18! I feel like we could spend our entire 31 days just on this Psalm and we would still not exhaust our study! What a wonderful treasure trove of reminders of all that our God is and wants to be to us! *Psalm 18:30 (NLT) God's way is perfect. All the LORD's promises prove true. He is a shield for all who look to him for protection.* Is He who we look to for protection? Are His promises that which we run to first to secure our minds and hearts in the wind and waves of this world? God's way is perfectly flawless and flawed as we are He longs to be our Strength, Rock, Fortress, Savior, God, protector,

Shield, Power, Safety… He is the I AM (see Exodus 3:14) all that we would ever need. Jesus is enough. In trusting obedience we find peace. Psalm 18:39 tells us God has armed us with strength for the battle. Take a moment to read Hebrews 13:21 and 2 Timothy 3:16-17. God makes us fit to flourish! Are we fitting time with Him into our day?!! The latter part of Psalm 18:39 reminds us God subdues our enemies under our feet. Our Conquering, Victorious King is *far above all rule and authority, power and dominion, and every name that is invoked, not only in the present age but also in the one to come. Ephesians 1:21 (NIV) But thanks be to God! He gives us the victory through our Lord Jesus Christ. 1 Corinthians 15:57 (NIV)* Dear one, on this journey to our Heavenly Home we are equipped with victory in Jesus our Savior! Do not forfeit ground (especially the real-estate in your mind) to the enemy that God has already won for you! Do not let your circumstances frame your perspective but rather His love displayed for you on the cross and His power available to you through His resurrection (see Ephesians 1:17-23 and Romans 8:31-39)!

- I love Psalm 19! It speaks to the power and beauty of God's creation. *For since the creation of the world God's invisible qualities - his eternal power and divine nature - have been clearly seen, being understood from what has been made, so that people are without excuse. Romans 1:20 (NIV)* I pray for my loved ones and myself included the Scripture in Matthew 13:16 (NIV), *But blessed are your eyes because they see, and your ears because they hear.* I never want to be so busy I miss His love notes written all around me in His creation! By verses 7-10 in

Psalm 19 it seems to switch focus from creation to the beauty of God's Word! Looking back over those few verse we are reminded we won't find treasure like that in this world. *Those who look to him are radiant; their faces are never covered with shame. Psalm 34:5 (NIV)* His Word offers more than any world beauty treatment and the effects are guaranteed! Highly valuable (Psalm 19:10) and yet available for free to us all. *For God so loved the world that he gave his one and only Son, that whoever believes in him shall not perish but have eternal life. John 3:16 (NIV)* God speaks through His creation and His Word however as Psalm 19:12-14 indicates to me, the Word desires a relationship and through His Word we find it! *In the beginning was the Word, and the Word was with God, and the Word was God. He was with God in the beginning. Through him all things were made; without him nothing was made that has been made. In him was life, and that life was the light of all mankind. The light shines in the darkness, and the darkness has not overcome it. John 1:1-5 (NIV)* We cannot do this world on our own, but why would we even try to when we have the Light of Life dear one!?!!

- Psalm 20:1 references God by the name of the God of Jacob. Jacob struggled in life and wrestled with God. He experienced life change through his relationship with God and one such indicator was Jacob's name change by God, to Israel. (This name change came about through a wrestling match between Jacob and God - see Genesis 32.) Jacob's character was deceitful and tricky however God renamed him Israel, or triumphant with God. When Psalm 20:1 (NIV) begins with, *May the LORD answer you when you are in distress…* Jacob knew distress, and not just caused by others but also distress brought on by himself; and yet God did not write him off, He re-wrote his story. *Psalm 20:7 (NIV) Some trust in chariots and some in horses, but we trust in the name of the LORD our God.* The Name above all names, the Name that redeems, restores and refreshes to be fit to flourish! *Do not gloat over me, my enemy! Though I have fallen, I will rise. Though I sit in darkness, the LORD will be my light. Micah 7:8 (NIV)*

"Cool Down": Record the coolest thing God gifted you that you would like to really root your life down into; that through your reception of His Truth, you will grow… truly fit to flourish!

_____

_____

_____

_____

_____

_____

_____

Thank you dearly for joining me today on this journey! See you tomorrow!!

~ DAY 5 ~

Date: _____

Hi! High five, day five!! Well done! I feel like Samuel in 1 Samuel 7:12 (NIV); like we should set down some kind of mile marker to celebrate our progress or something! *Then Samuel took a stone and set it up between Mizpah and Shen. He named it Ebenezer, saying, "Thus far the LORD has helped us."* Oh He has, He has! Praise Him! The joy of the Lord is our strength (Nehemiah 8:10)!

Warm Up and Worship: Do you feel a reason to praise our God welling up in your soul too? Please record one reason your heart finds joy in God our Savior today.

_____

_____

Pray Scripture: *Restore to me the joy of your salvation and grant me a willing spirit, to sustain me. Psalm 51:12 (NIV)* Please continue in a time of personal prayer between you and the Lord.

P.R. & P.R.

_____

_____

_____

_____

_____

_____

_____

_____

_____

_____

Daily Devotional Reading: "Building A Relationship"

He replied, "Because you have so little faith. Truly I tell you, if you have faith as small as a mustard seed, you can say to this mountain, 'Move from here to there,' and it will move. Nothing will be impossible for you."
Matthew 17:20 (NIV)

It's not about the size of your faith but rather where you place it.

After the disciple Peter, declares Jesus to be the Messiah, Jesus responds, *And I tell you that you are Peter, and on this rock I will build my church, and the gates of Hades will not overcome it. Matthew 16:18 (NIV)*

Peter makes an amazing declaration of faith, placing every ounce of faith he had been given, on Jesus as the Scriptures promised Messiah! Peter had decided that Jesus would be the foundation of his life, his Rock of Truth. How does Jesus respond? Well, He didn't tell Peter he had to build the church, Jesus told Peter, HE HIMSELF would build… Jesus would build on Peter's faith; and NOTHING can overcome God's building plans in any life willing to place their faith in Jesus as their Savior (Jer. 29:11, Job 42:2, Phil. 1:6, Eph. 2:10, Jn. 3:16, Rom. 8:31-39). That is living hope!

Jesus isn't looking for perfection. He knew we could never attain such a status on our own which is why He went to the cross for us. Rather, Jesus is after a relationship with us and when was the last time any relationship you have EVER engaged in was 100% perfect?!

Relationships are built through persistent patience, trust, forgiveness, grace, mercy, humility… ANY of that sound easy? Now think of the types of situations that require those qualities… are they easy? Nope. However when you choose to enter into a relationship with your Heavenly Father who IS Perfection Himself 100% of the time, the odds of a beautiful relationship in spite of our own many messy failings and shortcomings is guaranteed, by His amazing grace!

Today, stop striving to be loved, to earn what God Almighty FREELY extends to you! Place your mustard seed of faith in Him who is strong enough to hold you firm and secure; Who longs to pull you close and build a relationship with you on the sure foundation of Himself. Come as you are, abide in His presence, submit to His love… and dear one, you just watch what He builds with your life as a display of His splendor!

The Spirit you received does not make you slaves, so that you live in fear again; rather, the Spirit you received brought about your adoption to sonship. And by him we cry, "Abba, Father." Romans 8:15 (NIV)

Study in the Psalms: Today we will be reading Psalms 21, 22, 23, 24 and 25.

- Converse with God as you read through each Psalm.
- Pause and reflect on verses that catch your heart's attention.
- Record one verse from each Psalm that holds impact for you.
- Review your list. Is there a theme in the verses you highlighted? Take time and listen for God's voice to your heart.

- My favorite verse from Psalm 21:

  _____

  _____

  _____

- My favorite verse from Psalm 22:

  _____

  _____

  _____

- My favorite verse from Psalm 23:

  _____

  _____

  _____

- My favorite verse from Psalm 24:

  _____

  _____

  _____

- My favorite verse from Psalm 25:

  _____

_____

_____

Five points God pulled out for me as I pondered over our Scripture reading today. I do wish we were actually together with a cup of coffee (black) and some chocolate (dark chocolate) so we could truly share both ways! What would your order be for our little chat?

- Psalm 21 gives a wonderful example of a grateful heart. The first half is all focused on praising God for who He is and what He has done! Obviously the psalmist confidence lies in God Almighty. When we are confident that our blessings, our gifts, talents, time, energy, finances are all from God we will be more willing to humbly and freely give them away. Serving with our gifts brings glory and honor to the Gift Giver. *In the same way, let your light shine before others, that they may see your good deeds and glorify your Father in heaven. Matthew 5:16 (NIV)* This leads to the second half of the Psalm in which confidence is declared in what God will do! One thing verse 11 reminds us is that God will not allow evil to win in the end! Hallelujah! In the meanwhile before the ultimate victory is brought about and we are trudging through what at times feels like the thickets, we still have hope! We still can choose joy! Even in the pain and tears we can choose hope and joy for verse 4 reminds me we have the gift of eternal life! We have Living Hope! *and whoever lives by believing in me will never die. Do you believe this?" John 11:26 (NIV) Praise be to God and Father of our Lord Jesus Christ! In his great mercy he has given us new birth into a living hope though the resurrection of*

Jesus Christ from the dead, 1 Peter 1:3 (NIV) We have Living Hope that sustains when we feel the strains of being a living sacrifice; *Therefore, I urge you, brothers and sisters, in view of God's mercy, to offer your bodies as a living sacrifice, holy and pleasing to God — this is your true and proper worship. Romans 12:1 (NIV)* Psalm 21:7 reminds us we have the unfailing love of the Most High!! The Most High loves you without fail! Let that Truth sink in. There is no greater love, you have the attention and affection of the Most High!!! If we keep our focus on Truth we are unshakable! The enemy can't get through with lies that will work on someone rooted and convinced they have the unfailing love of the Most High God. Verse 6 also reminds us we have His presence with us always and what joy (even in the tears and the pain) we can choose to embrace within the depths of our soul because we are not alone. In all that we face we are never alone in Jesus. Last thought on this Psalm before we move on is that verse 2 finds praise in having one's heart's desires met. *Take delight in the Lord, and he will give you the desires of your heart. Psalm 37:4 (NIV)* When our delight is in God our desires will align with His. *Do not be conformed to the pattern of this world, but be transformed by the renewing of you mind. Then you will be able to test and approve what God's will is — his good, pleasing and perfect will. Romans 12:2 (NIV)* God's will is always good, pleasing and perfect even if at times it many not FEEL like it. Feelings are not facts. In the Garden Jesus prayed that salvation might come to us a different way than through Him on the cross and yet through prayer Jesus allowed His heart to be aligned with the Heavenly Fathers perfect way; and we were saved! *"Father, if you are willing, take this cup from me; yet not my will but yours be done." Luke 22:42 (NIV)*

- What a perfect verse to move us into the topic of Psalm 22! As you have noticed it is quite difficult, near impossible to keep the treasures mined through the Psalms to a minimal five points each day!! However that is one of the beautiful things about Scripture there is always, always, always something more to uncover! *Call to me and I will answer you and tell you great and unsearchable things you do not know.' Jeremiah 33:3 (NIV)* I like to call that verse reference "God's phone number"! Psalm 22:1 record's what Jesus called out from the cross (see Matthew 27:46). The agony of the cross is separation from God which Jesus bore on our behalf. He took our sin and shame upon His shoulders, endured the punishment once for all time that we might receive forgiveness and reconciliation to God forever!!! *For the wages of sin is death, but the gift of God is eternal life in Christ Jesus our Lord. Romans 6:23 (NIV)* Psalm 22:30-31 speaks of future generations (of which we are included) that will be made known of what He has done and we are to proclaim it further into the future! You are an important piece of the plan and what He has started He is sure to bring to a flourishing finish dear one! Keep on in our Mighty Conquering Victorious Warrior King! *being confident of this, that he who began a good work in you will carry it on to completion until the day of Christ Jesus. Philippians 1:6 (NIV)*

- Psalm 23 is about our Good Guiding Shepherd. He gave His life to lead us faithfully in ours, that we might bring Him glory and honor as we journey Home; even as He extends His Kingdom, our

Home, through us! Amazing grace!! Psalm 23:3 tells us He restores or refreshes our souls. Our souls are made up of our minds and emotions and no one, no thing can pull us back together, restored and refreshed mentally, emotionally like our God who knit us together in the first place (Psalm 139). He knows and understands the parts of you, you don't even know exist, let alone understand! I appreciate that verse 4 states we walk *through* the darkest valley. In Jesus no one has to *stay* there! Our Good Shepherd will faithfully lead us through all the way Home where we will dwell forever. Verse 5 talks about a table prepared for me among my enemies! I'd personally prefer to eat elsewhere wouldn't you?! But it's when we commune with Jesus, remembering His death on the cross and His resurrection from the grave that we are reminded no enemy can overcome those of us in Him! We can eat, sleep, do life in pure peace dear one, even in the presence of our enemies!

- As we believe on Jesus' death on the cross in our place and begin to walk in relationship that grows even through the valleys of our lives, we gain confidence of His sure return! Psalm 24 reminds us of His ultimate reign forever more! He is our King of kings and yet He extends us a crown! Psalm 21:3 spoke of it, 1 Peter 5:4, 1 Corinthians 9:25 and James 1:12 also make reference to the victors crown God extends to those who keep the faith, enduring in the race He has marked out for us through the finish line! In the end we will want that crown because we will want to participate in such worship as Revelation 4:10-11 (NIV) depicts for us! *the twenty-four elders fall down before him who sits on the throne and worship him who lives for ever and ever. They lay their crowns before the throne and say: "You are worthy, our Lord and God, to receive glory and honor and power, for you created all things, and by your will they were created and have their being."*

- It is possible that David wrote this Psalm during the time Absalom (David's son) was rebelling against him. If you can only imagine the pain and heartache heaped upon hopelessness! It's easy to loose hope when we feel we have no options left, we are clear out of control, to help, save, fix… However David begins this Psalm 25 declaring a rightly placed trust. Not in himself but in the One who is always in control! Our God is a God of order not chaos (look at creation and the unfolding of it in Genesis) and He holds all things together always!! (See also 1 Corinthians 14:40 and Colossians 1:17) Psalm 25:2 finds David asking God not to let him be put to shame because a lack of hope brings shame and Paul wrote in Romans 5:5 that the hope we have in our God does not put us to shame! Psalm 25:21 finds David declaring his hope to be in God. Not only has David rightly placed his trust but also his hope and now, even in his anguish he can see above the gloom of his own dark clouds clearly enough to end his prayer praying for others… *Deliver Israel, O God, from all their troubles! Psalm 25:22 (NIV)* Incredible right! It's true what is said in Isaiah 58:10 (NIV) *and if you spend yourself in behalf of the hungry and satisfy the needs of the oppressed, then your light will rise in the darkness, and your night will become like the noonday.* The fastest way down is introspection but look out and things are sure to start looking up!

"Cool Down": Please record the most prominent Truth God produced and placed on your heart today to bring you peace. *For he himself is our peace... Ephesians 2:14 (NIV)*

_____

_____

_____

_____

_____

_____

God bless you muchly~

~ DAY 6 ~

Date: _____

Welcome! Yesterday I did actually have a physical work out that has me feeling most muscles in my body today quite prominently; every time I move. The workout, if you are wondering, was called "intense infinity tag". It was with a group of elementary children. However my ache has made me grateful because it means I'm still alive and with feeling. Bent over and sucking wind into searing lungs yesterday had me questioning at times if it might end differently for me. But His mercies are new every morning and I'm back!

Warm Up and Worship: What makes you grateful for His new mercies today (Lamentations 3:22-23)?

_____

_____

Pray Scripture: *In the morning, Lord, you hear my voice; in the morning I lay my requests before you and wait expectantly. Psalm 5:3 (NIV)* Please continue in prayer as you begin your time with the ultimate Romancer of your soul.

P.R. & P.R.

_____

_____

_____

_____

_____

_____

_____

_____

_____

Daily Devotional Reading: "Go Play"

...(Our God, however, turned the curse into a blessing.)
Nehemiah 13:2 (NIV)

As summer trickles to an end with back to school signs looming overhead, quite literally everywhere; I find myself doing a little end-of-summer cleaning. It seems in life, we are always editing, revising, scrubbing, repainting, remodeling, reloading, refreshing... If it were only just so easy to use that little "magic eraser" on real life mistakes and blunders, right?!

Our God came to earth to do more than a little cleaning; He came to set in motion a plan to make all things new... NEW! *He who was seated on the throne said, "I am making everything new!" Then he said, "Write this down, for these words are trustworthy and true."* Revelation 21:5 (NIV) Dear one, we have WAY more than just a fresh coat of paint to look forward to in Jesus!!

Nehemiah 13:2 depicts a mighty blunder and yet ends with a treasure tucked inside a parentheses; like the author knew a special secret! Maybe you've been there too... yes, the mistake was massive, the failure fracturing, the catastrophe colossal… maybe you just feel like you have hit a pause in life; quite literally a pothole?! Could it be the Author of your life is inserting parentheses; a moment to look up and breathe; to receive Truth?!!

You might want to take notes because this one is trustworthy and true! (*Our God turns curses into blessings, *valleys of trouble into doors of hope, **harm, into good that saves many lives!) Let's rest in that whisper of Truth. Living Hope exists on every page of life. Now maybe put down the scrub brush, that "magic eraser", and go play in these last sprinkles of summer!

Here is the sea, great and wide, which teems with creatures innumerable, living things both small and great. There go the ships, and Leviathan, which you formed to play in it. Psalm 104:25-26 (ESV)

Dear one, have fun, let His Truth wash over you and go play!

See: *Hosea 2:15, **Genesis 50:20 and Revelation 22:3

~~~

Study in the Psalms: Today we will be reading Psalms 26, 27, 28, 29 and 30.

- Converse with God as you read through each Psalm.
- Pause and reflect on verses that catch your heart's attention.
- Record one verse from each Psalm that holds impact for you.
- Review your list. Is there a theme in the verses you highlighted? Take time and listen for God's voice to your heart.

- My favorite verse from Psalm 26:

  _____

  _____

  _____

- My favorite verse from Psalm 27:

  _____

  _____

  _____

- My favorite verse from Psalm 28:

  _____

  _____

  _____

- My favorite verse from Psalm 29:

  _____

  _____

  _____

- My favorite verse from Psalm 30:

  _____

  _____

  _____

Five additional points to ponder, if you will.

- Psalm 26:1 finds David declaring a blameless life. None of us lives sinless, we are human and that is impossible. However as we make it a habit to walk with God day in and day out, continually communing with Him at the cross, regularly confessing our sins in sincerity, asking to be searched thoroughly for anything we may have missed; any rouge motives, ill intent, vain conceit, foolish pride… we can walk clean, covered in His blood soaked robes of righteousness. *I delight greatly in the Lord; my soul rejoices in my God. For he has clothed me with garments of salvation and arrayed me in a robe of his righteousness… Isaiah 61:10 (NIV)* Literally blameless, for *as far as the east is from the west, so far has he removed our transgressions from us. Psalm 103:12 (NIV)*

- Psalm 27:2 declares the stronghold we want, the only stronghold that can truly free us and or keep us from addictions that hold us strong. In the life and death trials of life that could threaten to bind us in fear we have *Philippians 1:21 (NIV) For to me, to live is Christ and to die is gain.*; so even if the worst happens and we go down, we go up! Up to heaven!! There is no defeat for those in Jesus, none!! *Because God's children are human beings —made of flesh and blood— the Son also became flesh and blood. For only as a human being could he die, and only by dying could he break the power of the devil, who had the power of death. Only in this way could he set us free all who have lived their lives as slaves to the fear of dying. Hebrews 2:14-15 (NLT)* Psalm 27:1 declares our God to be our light. L.ife I.n G.od H.olds T.ruth - Amen! He is our Light and salvation! What is more fearful than the dark unknown and yet darkness is as light to Him (Psalm 139:12) and even in the worst we have His saving life! Dear one, we have nothing to fear in Jesus, nothing! The continual challenge is to allow our faith to grow so that fear cannot penetrate and pull our focus from His face, His Truth. Choosing to continually turn from fear and focus toward the One who has never turned from us, increases our trust as we find Him faithful in His timing, teaching, tactics… all of it! knowing it is always what is best because He understands things we can't and knows things we don't. We can choose Psalm 27:6, to sacrifice with shouts of joy. Sometimes choosing praise is the hardest thing and yet God is our warrior through worship. In all we don't know or understand we can choose to offer a sacrifice of praise with shouts of joy. Maybe not because our current situation is joyful but we do have a Heavenly Home in Jesus we are headed to that is full of everlasting joy. *Wait for the LORD; be strong and take heart and wait for the LORD. Psalm 27:14 (NIV)* In the meantime, *My heart says of you, "Seek his face!" Your face, LORD, I will seek!" Psalm 27:8 (NIV)* Because if we recall back to *Psalm 24:5-6 (NIV) They will receive blessing from the LORD and vindication from God their Savior. Such is the generation of those who seek him, who seek your face, God of Jacob.*

• When we see in the Psalms prayers for the enemy to be dealt with harshly I want it to remind me to pray that no tolerance be made for the things in me that are contrary to God's likeness. I want God to rip out the things in my life that bear no fruit that I might look more like His Son. Psalm 28:5 speaks of disregard for the things God has done. *Romans 1:21 (NIV) For although they knew God, they neither glorified him as God nor gave thanks to him, but their thinking became futile and their foolish hearts were darkened.* A darkened heart for lack of gratitude! Yikes! May we heed the warning.

- *Psalm 29:10-11 (NIV) The LORD sits enthroned over the flood; the LORD is enthroned as King forever. The LORD gives strength to his people; the LORD blesses his people with peace.* Dear one, over whatever floods your heart today may the Truth that He is enthroned over it, flood your mind with peace. *He says, "Be still, and know that I am God; I will be exalted among the nations, I will be exalted in the earth." Psalm 46:10 (NIV)* Psalm 29 describes the awesome power of His voice. So powerful verse 5 states that it could break the cedars of Lebanon! Those trees could be 30 feet around and about 120 feet tall!!! How much power and volume are you allowing His voice to have in and over your life? If you are a parent you have probably come to know your child was born with a gift… it's called "selective hearing"… we're all born with it!! So today, let's tune in to Truth.

- *…weeping may stay for the night, but rejoicing comes in the morning. Psalm 30:5 (NIV)* When I needed to be encouraged as a kid (maybe even still) my dad always said, "Don't worry the sun will still come up tomorrow… unless of course Jesus comes back." It always helped me put things in perspective. I could never make a mistake so big that would prevent God from being able to bring the hope of a new day. A fresh new beginning with no mistakes in it, like freshly fallen snow in the early morning with no footprints yet! *Lamentations 3:19-25 (NIV) I remember my affliction and my wandering, the bitterness and the gall. I well remember them, and my soul is downcast within me. Yet this I call to mind and therefore I have hope: Because of the Lord's great love we are not consumed, for his compassions never fail. They are new every morning; great is your faithfulness. I say to myself, "The Lord is my* *portion; therefore I will wait for him." The Lord is good to those whose hope is in him, to the one who seeks him;*

"Cool Down":

_____

_____

_____

_____

_____

_____

_____

Thanks for playing today! See you tomorrow!

~ DAY 7 ~

Date: _____

Welcome dear one. The number seven is the number of completion and though we are only just beginning our 31 day spiritual fitness challenge together, we have completed week one!! Well done! This morning I was headed to an address in 1 Corinthians when I found myself accidentally or maybe coincidentally in 2 Corinthians with a profound message! Actually someone once told me she thinks there are no coincidences, just God showing up unannounced. I like that thought and I sure felt His encouragement this morning on my detour through His Word and I thought it appropriate to share with you now. *2 Corinthians 8:11-12 (NIV) Now finish the work, so that your eager willingness to do it may be matched by your completion of it, according to your means. For if the willingness is there, the gift is acceptable according to what one has, not according to what one does not have.* Don't you just LOVE that!! It is so easy to become discouraged feeling like what you are doing is not enough and often because you feel YOU are not enough in some way or in all ways. But this verse is a perfect reminder that who God has made you to be and the desires He has stirred in your heart matters to Him! So, now finish the work dear one! The thing He has stirred an eagerness in your heart to do... do it! Full out with what you have, not worrying about what you don't have or what others will think or not think; you work for God and not man anyway (Colossians 3:23). Apart from God we have nothing and can do nothing (John 15:5) so if we are in Jesus, our Vine, what He has given us is enough to fulfill His purpose for our lives, His agenda for our day. In Jesus you are enough because Jesus is always, always enough and He says, … *be strong and immovable. Always work enthusiastically for the Lord, for you know that nothing you do for the Lord is ever useless. 1 Corinthians 15:58 (NIV)* Goodness gracious you gotta love a good detour with the Lord! Amen! I already feel a warmth stirring in my soul let's get to our time of worship!

Warm Up with Worship:

_____

_____

Pray Scripture: *Not one of all the LORD's good promises to Israel failed; every one was fulfilled. Joshua 21:45 (NIV)* Dear Heavenly Father, You are trustworthy, help us to stand strong on your faithfulness. Please strengthen our hands, our hearts, our minds to remain steadfast upon the Rock of Truth - who You say You are in the Scriptures and have proven to be throughout time… please continue in prayer individually as we prepare our hearts to honor His leadership.

P.R. & P.R. (Prayer Requests & Praise Reports)

_____

_____

_____

_____

_____

_____

_____

_____

_____

Daily Devotional Reading: "Created For Acceptance"

John 3:16-17 (NIV)
For God so loved the world that he gave…

God showed His love through giving… giving Himself (2 Corinthians 8:9). Jesus is the greatest Gift we could ever receive.

(verse 16)…he gave his one and only Son, that whoever believes in him shall not perish but have eternal life.

We were created for acceptance. To accept Him as Savior and truly live!

(verse 17) For God did not send his Son into the world to condemn the world, but to save the world through him.

Jesus came not to condemn us but to save us. God loves us, wants us, is willing to accept us as His children if we will accept Jesus as our Lord and Savior. Our very beings were made to accept and be accepted. So in this world when we experience rejection and exclusion it can send us in a tailspin of hurt that either implodes or exudes from us in a million different shared and broken ways, that threaten to scar even those around us!

The only way to combat this tailspin is to keep Jesus as our first thought. Joseph set's a good example in Genesis 45:5-9. The wrong done to Joseph is recounted, yet combated, with a confident thought life given to God Almighty's good sovereign plan and hand working in and over his life! The key is a relationship built on trust. Trust that enables us to walk by faith and not sight (2 Corinthians 5:7) when we cannot seem to see God working in the background of our circumstances. Trust in His faithful Word that He is ALWAYS working (John 5:17) even at this very moment for the good of those that love Him (Romans 8:28) even if we cannot see or comprehend it (Proverbs 3:5-6).

Consider him who endured such opposition from sinners, so that you will not grow weary and lose heart. Hebrews 12:3 (NIV) "*If the world hates you, keep in mind that it hated me first. John 15:18 (NIV)* Jesus persevered by the power of the Holy Spirit to save us. "*The Spirit of the Lord is on me, because he has anointed me to proclaim good news to the poor. He has sent me to proclaim freedom for the prisoners and recovery of sight for the blind, to set the oppressed free, Luke 4:18 (NIV)*

Our God has equipped us with His Spirit, everything we need to overcome the rejection of this world as He accomplishes His purpose through us. *being confident of this, that he who began a good work in you will carry it on to completion until the day of Christ Jesus. Philippians 1:6 (NIV)* "*But blessed is the one who trusts in the LORD, whose confidence is in him. Jeremiah 17:7 (NIV)*

When we keep Jesus as our first thought in all situations, decisions, circumstances, reactions and yes, even when we experience rejections, we will find the strength to orient or reorient (if need be) on Truth. You and I were created for acceptance, an acceptance made possible through Christ's rejection. Never forget Who understands completely, our hurt in rejection (Hebrews 4:15). He is the One whose Spirit will sustain you as you do what you were created to do.

But you will receive power when the Holy Spirit comes on you; and you will be my witnesses in Jerusalem, and in all Judea and Samaria, and to the ends of the earth." Acts 1:8 (NIV) … And surely I am with you always, to the very end of the age." Matthew 28:20 (NIV)

You are deeply loved by God; accept The Truth.
You were made for great purpose; reflect The Truth for others to accept too.
How?... Keep Jesus as your first thought and follow His example (thought, word and action) set in His Word. Show His love through the giving of yourself in the strength He provides, not to condemn but rather that others might see His heart of love and acceptance through you and be saved by Truth (John 14:6).

So, my dear brothers and sisters, be strong and immovable. Always work enthusiastically for the Lord, for you know that nothing you do for the Lord is ever useless. 1 Corinthians 15:58 (NLT) I have told you these things, so that in me you may have peace. In this world you will have trouble. But take heart! I have overcome the world." John 16:33 (NIV) What, then, shall we say in response to these things? If God is for us, who can be against us? Romans 8:31 (NIV) No, in all these things we are more than conquerors through him who loved us. Romans 8:37 (NIV)

PS. How do we become MORE than a conquerer?! By using what the enemy meant to harm us, for good! Only by the grace of God can we be conquerers like that! *You intended to harm me, but God intended it for good to accomplish what is now being done, the saving of many lives. Genesis 50:20 (NIV)*

~~~

Study in the Psalms: Today we will be reading Psalms 31, 32, 33, 34 and 35.

- Converse with God as you read through each Psalm.
- Pause and reflect on verses that catch your heart's attention.
- Record one verse from each Psalm that holds impact for you.
- Review your list. Is there a theme in the verses you highlighted? Take time and listen for God's voice to your heart.

- My favorite verse from Psalm 31:

_____

_____

_____

- My favorite verse from Psalm 32:

_____

_____

_____

- My favorite verse from Psalm 33:

  _____

  _____

  _____

- My favorite verse from Psalm 34:

  _____

  _____

  _____

- My favorite verse from Psalm 35:

  _____

  _____

  _____

Five additional points to ponder from our Scripture passages today. (I know I say five points and it really probably reads as if there are 9 points within each bullet point! I truly am trying to keep the commentary to a minimum (insert embarrassed emoji face)!! The important part is just reading the Scriptures… if you don't get to my five(bazillion) follow up points, that's okay!!)

- Psalm 31:4 refers to a trap set for us. Yes the enemy is pursuing that which is valuable to God and as God's child the enemy will pursue you and I. However think back to Genesis in the garden of Eden when the promise was made by God that the enemy would not win in the end (see Genesis 3). Actually the enemy's head has been crushed as foretold in Genesis 3:15. Jesus won taking the cross and overcoming the grave! However just as a snakes body will continue to convulse even after the head is crushed for a bit (freaky I know) it cannot continue for long. In this world that has ultimately been overcome by our God still experiences the enemy's convulsing body (so to speak) but his time is short, our God is coming back and that will be the end of our enemy once and for all. So do not fall prey to a fallen and defeated predator. Stand firm in the victory already won! *Psalm 31:24 (NIV) Be strong and take heart, all you who hope in the LORD.* Psalm 31:5 records a statement Jesus spoke from the cross (Luke 23:46) committing His Spirit into the Father's hands. Stephan in Acts 7:59 while being martyred for the faith also committed himself into God's hands. Dear one, in His Almighty hands is always the safest place to be. *2 Timothy 4:18 (NIV) The Lord will rescue me from every evil attack and will bring me safely to his heavenly kingdom. To him be glory for ever and ever. Amen.* Sometimes it's not the enemy but our own evil desires that pull us off course. We make the enemy's job easy when we do not single-mindedly pursue God's righteousness. (See James 1:13-15 and 1 Corinthians 10:13) The rumors for whisperings of terror indicated in Psalm 31:13 is followed by a bold, *But I trust in you, LORD;* in verse 14 (NIV). Jesus experienced it too, see John 7:12 as just one example but see also verses 28-29 to see that Jesus confidently found His validation from Truth. It matters what we tune into as it has the power turn our life. Psalm 31:7, 22 also confirm God's care and attentiveness to our detail. We can truly rest in Him dear one. *The LORD directs the steps of the godly. He delights in every detail of their lives. Psalm 37:23 (NLT) Then Jesus said, "Let's go off by ourselves to a quiet place and rest awhile." ... Mark 6:31 (NLT)*

- Psalm 32:1 exclaims how blessed we are upon receiving forgiveness, and not just forgiveness for our accidental sins but also for our willful sins. How gracious is our God. Isaiah 52:12 in the NLT finishes with, *He bore the sins of many and interceded for rebels.* Another beautiful picture of the gracious and merciful heart of our Savior is found in John 8:1-11. If we want to look more like Jesus we need to put down our stones and extend forgiveness and grace to others from the overflow He has lavished on us. Psalm 32:8 is one of my favorite verses but I cannot forget to heed verse 9. God is willing to lead, I must be willing to follow if I'm going to head anywhere worthwhile!

- Psalm 33 just makes you want to stand to your feet and shout, "hallelujah and amen", right!! We are to praise Him for Truth, justice and His goodness. In a world of half-truths, injustice and evil we have much to praise God for in just who He is! All of creation speaks of His power, His Word is sustaining and has been since the beginning of time as we know it!! Remain daily in His Word and He will sustain you!!! Jesus is enough! Psalm 33:15 reminds us that the One who knit our individual heart together knows best how to service it dear one, run to Him and remain in Him!

- I had to laugh as I took a break from writing and during that time did some research on anti-aging creams... Only to come back to

Psalm 34:5 (NIV) previously highlighted in my Bible!! Just the timely reminder that I needed! God is so kind! *Those who look to him are radiant; their faces are never covered with shame.* The application of God's Truth to the lives we face daily, will work wonders for us, wonders not found in this world! Step one to application is to praise God at ALL times as Psalm 34:1 advices. How different does a life look when a spirit of praise is ever on ones lips?!! Psalm 34:6 indicates a saving from all troubles. In this world everyone has problems, but only believers have the Problem Solver. In Him we will lack no good thing (Psalm 34:10). We may not have everything we want but we will have everything we need. We will always have enough spiritual nourishment to sustain us. Psalm 34:8 says taste and see not see and taste. If we will take Him in faith we will experience Him in Truth. *Psalm 34:22 (NIV) The LORD will rescue his servants; no one who takes refuge in him will be condemned.* We are all invited to take refuge in Him… the choice is ours.

- Psalm 35 may seem harsh at first however I admire that the psalmist was leaving the issues at hand in God's hand rather than taking up vengeance himself. *Romans 12:19 (NIV) Do not take revenge, my dear friends, but leave room for God's wrath, for it is written: "It is mine to avenge; I will repay," says the Lord.* Delayed deliverance can be an agent of discouragement but we are wise to rest in God's perfect timing. A delay might be divine so delve into God's Word while we wait on the wonders God has prepared for those who love Him. *Romans 8:28 (NIV) And we know that in all things God works for the good of those who love him, who have been called according to his purpose.* Keep in mind *Ephesians 6:12 (NIV) For our struggle is not against flesh and blood, but against the rulers, against the authorities, against the powers of this dark world and against the spiritual forces of evil in the heavenly realms.* When the enemy turns his "spear", his fiery darts on us in any of his various forms, remember Jesus took a spear in His side on the cross. Don't let the enemy accuse you falsely. Yes, he will accuse you and be very convincing because you also know yourself... but remind him of the whole Truth! *So if the Son sets you free, you will be free indeed. John 8:36 (NIV) no weapon forged against you will prevail, and you will refute every tongue that accuses you. This is the heritage of the servants of the LORD, and this is their vindication from me,"* *declares the LORD. Isaiah 54:17 (NIV)*

"Cool Down": Record what you learned today that will help you keep calm, cool and collected in this crazy world.

_____

_____

_____

_____

_____

_____

_____

God bless you muchly~

~ DAY 8 ~

Date: _____

Hello! Today I experienced the thrill of worshiping at church while two of my children participated in the worship band together. *I have no greater joy than to hear that my children are walking in the truth. 3 John 1:4 (NIV)* I've watched them grow and listened to their many practices so to experience the fruit of their efforts in such a way this morning was a blessing beyond words. The time just ushered my heart into such a spirit of worship of our good, good God! Can you imagine what worship will be like in Heaven with all of God's children having a part in the band and choir?!! We worship our God because of His worth-ship… He is so worth it and we can worship in so many different ways throughout our days. As we will study today in the Psalms, David worshiped through a heart of reverence even in what felt like the worst of times.

Warm Up with Worship: Record how you can offer God your worship today just because at all times, in all things, He is still worth it.

_____

_____

Pray Scripture: *We wait in hope for the Lord; he is our help and our shield. In him our hearts rejoice, for we trust in his holy name. May your unfailing love be with us, Lord, even as we put our hope in you. Psalm 33:20-22 (NIV)* Please continue in prayer with God to begin your time in His Word.

P.R. & P.R.

_____

_____

_____

_____

_____

_____

_____

_____

_____

_____

Daily Devotional Reading: "Rise On The Rock"

The rain came down, the streams rose, and the winds blew and beat against that house; yet it did not fall, because it had its foundation on the rock.
Matthew 7:25 (NIV)

When all you see are wild waves and all you hear is whipping winds, doubts can begin to threaten your total drowning! In a lifeguarding class I learned that swimmers threatened by drowning rarely relax upon their rescue's arrival. Rather, they panic and cling to their rescuer to the point everyone's survival is in jeopardy!

Matthew 7:24-29 describes two homes within two identical storms. In one scenario the home is destroyed; in the other, the home is just fine! Same severe storm yet very different outcomes! To bring this illustration home, let's make "home" represent any part of our lives such as our families, friendships, careers, hopes and dreams... Now, how do we make sure our "home" makes it out of life's storms without crashing down?! According to this passage in Matthew the key is in what we tune into.

We can let the cause and effect of life's storm (the wind and waves) consume our focus OR we can focus our mind on the Words of God. If our mind holds the seed of Truth, it will begin to grow our emotions, which will bloom into action. Therefore everyone who hears these words of mine and puts them into practice is like a wise man who built his house on the rock. (verse 24) God is our Rock. He has given us great and precious promises to cast our anchor of sure hope into so that when the storms come (and they will come - (John 16:33)) we can emerge stronger, rooted on the rock solid foundation of God's trustworthy promises! (Colossians 3:1-2, Hebrews 12:1-3, 2 Peter 1:4, Hebrews 6:19)

James 4:7 (NIV) Submit yourselves, then, to God. Resist the devil, and he will flee from you. This is a promise that can bring peace to our peril. Resist the enemy, of your heart, mind, soul, home... and he will flee! Praise God who has made us vessels of His overcoming strength and victory! The power to resist the enemy is found in humble submission to Almighty God. (1 Peter 5:6-8, Philippians 4:7)

A drowning victim risks his rescue fighting to save himself when actually his saving would come in humble submission, in laying still within the rescue swimmer's arms. We too will find the strength to sustain us in any of life's storms through choosing to submit and trust God. Submission is anything but a passive move. It takes more strength to submit than to assert your own will. We see Jesus exemplify this strength in the Garden of Gethsemane as he heads to the cross for us. Mark 14:36 (NIV) states, *"Abba, Father," he said, "everything is possible for you. Take this cup from me. Yet not what I will, but what you will."*

Submitting to God's will, His way and His timing will require trust and a choice made over and over again to align our will with His higher one. The effect of this kind of living causes a "home" to be rooted on the sure foundation of Truth, and this "home" will not fall. (Isaiah 55:8-9)

Let the Truth you know, soak down into your soul. Anchor your foundation on the Rock that chose to rise in the midst of His greatest storm so that we wouldn't have to come crashing down in ours. Rise on the Rock dear one.

God is within her, she will not fall; God will help her at break of day. ... He says, "Be still and know that I am God;... Psalm 46:5,10 (NIV) For I am the LORD your God who takes hold of your right hand and says to you, Do not fear; I will help you. Isaiah 41:13 (NIV) I am leaving you with a gift-peace of mind and heart. And the peace I give is a gift the world cannot give. So don't be troubled or afraid. John 14:27 (NLT) The light shines in the darkness, and the darkness can never extinguish it. John 1:5 (NLT)

Study in the Psalms: Today we will be reading Psalms 36, 37, 38, 39 and 40.

- Converse with God as you read through each Psalm.
- Pause and reflect on verses that catch your heart's attention.
- Record one verse from each Psalm that holds impact for you.
- Review your list. Is there a theme in the verses you highlighted? Take time and listen for God's voice to your heart.

- My favorite verse from Psalm 36:

_____

_____

_____

- My favorite verse from Psalm 37:

_____

_____

_____

- My favorite verse from Psalm 38:

_____

_____

_____

- My favorite verse from Psalm 39:

_____

_____

_____

- My favorite verse from Psalm 40:

_____

_____

_____

Five additional points to ponder from our Scripture passages today.

• Psalm 36 reminds me of James 1:21 (NIV) which states, *Therefore, get rid of all moral filth and the evil that is so prevalent and humbly accept the word planted in you, which can save you.* Psalm 36:1-4 depicts the wicked that have no fear of God, a people that have somehow missed the awe and wonder of verses 5-8! Why?; because as Psalm 36:9 (NIV) states, *For with you is the fountain of life; in your light we see light.* As James 1:21 reminds us, it's in humbly accepting the Word that can save us from our own evil selves headed for our own demise due to our own prideful undoing! God's invitation to His House, to come under His wing is for all people (Psalm 36:7 NLT) and yet we see in Luke 13:34 that is an invite many sadly refuse. Psalm 36:5 (NLT) *Your unfailing love, O LORD, is as vast as the heavens;* … He cares for people and animals alike (Psalm 36:6, Matthew 10:29)! There is nothing that compares to our God and His love for us. Today let's pray that the foot of pride not take a foothold in our hearts and minds. *Jeremiah 2:13 (NIV) "My people have committed two sins: They have forsaken me, the spring of living water, and have dug their own cisterns, broken cisterns that cannot hold water. John 4:14 (NIV) but whoever drinks the water I give them will never thirst. Indeed, the water I give them will become in them a spring of water welling up to eternal life." Proverbs 1:7 (NIV) The fear of the LORD is the beginning of knowledge, but fools despise wisdom and instruction.*

- When I overview the beginning of the first 8 verse of Psalm 37 in my NIV Bible I see a message to my heart that reads like this: Do not fret, Trust in the LORD, Take delight int he LORD, Commit your way to the LORD, Be still before the LORD and wait patiently for Him, Refrain from anger, do not fret. Trust, Delight, Commit, Rest… all framed with don't worry! Don't be confused dear one, when we view the evil in this world. God has the upper hand and His plan, which includes His children, prevails in the end! *Psalm 37:9 (NIV) For those who are evil will be destroyed, but those who hope in the LORD will inherit the land.* As we journey remember *Philippians 2:13 (NIV) now it is God who works in you to will and to act in order to fulfill his good purpose.* So, *Do not withhold good from those to whom it is due, when it is in your power to act. Proverbs 3:27 (NIV)* We don't want to miss the ways He longs to delight our hearts as we delight in Him.

- *Psalm 38:13-15 (NLT) But I am deaf to all their threats. I am silent before them as one who cannot speak. I choose to hear nothing, and I make no reply. For I am waiting for you, O LORD.* … Reminds me of Luke 23:9-10 (NIV) just before Jesus' crucifixion Herod … *plied him with many questions, but Jesus gave him no answer. The chief priests and the teachers of the law were standing there, vehemently accusing him.* And *1 Peter 2:21-24 (NIV) To this you were called, because Christ suffered for you, leaving you an example, that you should follow in his steps. "He committed no sin, and no deceit was found in his mouth." When they hurled their insults at him, he did not retaliate; when he suffered, he made no threats. Instead, he entrusted himself to him who judges justly. "He himself bore our sins" in his body on the cross, so that we might die to sins and live for righteousness; "By his wounds you have been healed."* It seems in this Psalm David is suffering due to his own sin. His suffering is made worse by both friends that have turned on him as well as his enemies that are seizing an opportunity to kick him while he is down. David however continues to trust and rely on God's faithfulness. David does not deny his guilt but rather confesses it (vs. 4). David does not refute his punishment for his sin but rather asks that he not be punished in God's anger (vs.1), counting on God's mercy (vs. 15). Because of Jesus sacrifice on the cross we can receive mercy and grace - complete forgiveness - through an offer of a sincere and repentant heart. *Let us then approach God's throne of grace with confidence, so that we may receive mercy and find grace to help us in our time of need. Hebrews 4:16 (NIV)*

• In Psalm 39 David is troubled yet instead of spouting his feelings to all within hearing range David brings all to God. We don't need to be afraid to bringing our authentic feelings to God - He is already well aware and can handle us. In this Psalm along with Psalm 73:15 we see the effort to keep the negativity and complaining to the One who has the answers and the help we need. When we cast our complaints around we run the risk of derailing other's faith. *If I had spoken out like that, I would have betrayed your children. When I tried to understand all this, it troubled me deeply till I entered the sanctuary of God; then I understood their final destiny. Psalm 73:15-17 (NIV)* When in distress over God's ways allow Him the benefit of the doubt. His infinite mind has a deeper understanding of our life than our finite mind can comprehend. Bring your frustration to Him first allowing Him to fix your mind forward in faith. Life is too short to waste it wondering what if or why that or how come this... *Psalm 39:5 (NIV) ... Everyone is but a breath, even those who seem secure.* None of us is guaranteed the next moment let alone the next day or even year! (See Luke 12:13-21, Ecclesiastes 2:18) *Why, you do not even know what will happen tomorrow. What is your life? You are a mist that appears for a little while and then vanishes. James 4:14 (NIV)* Dear one, let's determine to make the most of our mist rather than miss it all together toiling in things that won't matter in eternity.

- Psalm 40:5 (NIV) is the list our minds need to rest on when we cannot sleep at night! *Many, LORD my God, are the wonders you have done, the things you planned for us. None can compare with you; were I to speak and tell of your deeds, they would be too many to declare.* Verse 6 (NIV) is also a prayer of mine, ... *but my ears you have opened ...* the NLT states it this way ... *Now that you have made me listen, I finally understand - ...* Oh that God would make me listen, open my ears and my mind that I might understand and live in obedient trust! *Psalm 40:8 (NIV) I desire to do your will, my God; your law is within my heart."* Let's continue on in His Word that He might have the time to write it within our hearts! The beginning of this Psalm relays blessings for waiting on the Lord. A lifting up, a setting firm, a giving of a new song, a spirit of praise and then the influence of such a faith reaches outward! Psalm 40:4 relays the blessing of waiting on and trusting God rather than giving in to the temptation of turning to the things of this world that boast quick fixes. *So do not throw away your confidence; it will be richly rewarded. Hebrews 10:35 (NIV)*

"Cool Down":

_____

_____

_____

_____

_____

_____

_____

God bless you muchly my dear sweet friend~

~ DAY 9 ~

Date: _____

Hello and welcome back! Yesterday we mentioned that our lives are but a mist and thus with every gifted spritz, or moment, we ought to make the most of it! James 4:14 (NIV) *Why, you do not even know what will happen tomorrow. What is your life? You are a mist that appears for a little while and then vanishes.* So, without further ado let's do just that! #makethemostofthemist

Warm Up and Worship:

_____

_____

Pray Scripture: *Do not be anxious about anything, but in every situation, by pryer and petition, with thanksgiving, present your requests to God. And the peace of God, which transcends all understanding, will guard your hearts and your minds in Christ Jesus. Philippians 4:6-7 (NIV)* Dear Heavenly Father thank you for peace that extends beyond our comprehension and that has the ability to guard our minds and hearts. Help us to receive that gift today as we roll all our cares onto Your, much more capable shoulders, in prayer… Please continue opening your time with the Lord in prayer.

P.R. & P.R.

_____

_____

_____

_____

_____

_____

_____

_____

_____

_____

Daily Devotional Reading: "'I'm Convinced!'"

But when they told him everything Joseph had said to them, and when he saw the carts Joseph had sent to carry him back, the spirit of their father Jacob revived. And Israel said, "I'm convinced! My son Joseph is still alive. I will go and see him before I die." Genesis 45:27-28 (NIV)

I wrestled a while with why the above verses used both names for the third patriarch. Why not just say, …the spirit of their father Jacob revived. And Jacob said... OR the spirit of their father Israel revived. And Israel said… Why use both his old name and the new name God had given him after emerging blessed through a wrestling match held in Genesis 32?! Then it hit me and I too felt like I emerged with a blessing having wrestled with this wondering thought for a day!!

The old self, Jacob, had become downcast, distraught, distressed over life's events YET having received a refreshing word, his spirit was revived and who emerges from the rubble refreshed, renewed and revived?!!! ISRAEL! The overcomer, just as God had declared him to be during that first wrestling match chapters ago!! *The law of the LORD is perfect, refreshing the soul. The statues of the LORD are trustworthy, making wise the simple. Psalm 19:7 (NIV)*

Dear one, the sacrificial blood of Jesus speaks a better Word than our world's system! May your spirit and my spirit be refreshed this very morning, absolutely convinced by the Spirit of the living God within us that Jesus is still alive!!! Hope lives!!!

May His Word elevate our thoughts and move us to respond to His better Word over the world's diagnosis of our life, our situation, our circumstances and relationships…!! By the power of His Word may we be moved to "go and see" Him too, working and moving this very moment in and through all things for the good of those who love Him!

For I am convinced that neither death nor life, neither angels nor demons, neither the present nor the future, nor any powers, neither height nor depth, nor anything else in all creation, will be able to separate us from the love of God that is in Christ Jesus our Lord. Romans 8:38-39 (NIV)

In our Living Christ, our Hope Eternal, Jesus, who loves you, you are more than a conquer dear one; more than a conquer - I'm convinced!

Study in the Psalms: Today we will be reading Psalms 41, 42, 43, 44 and 45.

- Converse with God as you read through each Psalm.
- Pause and reflect on verses that catch your heart's attention.
- Record one verse from each Psalm that holds impact for you.
- Review your list. Is there a theme in the verses you highlighted? Take time and listen for God's voice to your heart.

- My favorite verse from Psalm 41:

_____

_____

_____

- My favorite verse from Psalm 42:

_____

_____

_____

- My favorite verse from Psalm 43:

_____

_____

_____

- My favorite verse from Psalm 44:

_____

_____

_____

- My favorite verse from Psalm 45:

  _____

  _____

  _____

Five additional points to ponder from our Scripture passages today. But first, I've been thinking that if we were to record all of the treasures within these Psalms I think we might have to declare just as John did in John 21:25 (NIV), _Jesus did many other things as well. If every one of them were written down, I suppose that even the whole world would not have room for the books that would be written._ There may not be a book around with a binding big enough for us to hold all the treasures within these Psalms!! However, what John said about what WAS recorded, is my prayer for what little has been recorded over His Word in this little devotional. _John 20:31 (NIV) But these are written the you may believe that Jesus is the Messiah, the Son of God, and that by believing you may have life in his name._

- Psalm 41 will conclude the first of the five books of the Psalms. Psalm 41 begins with a blessing for those mindful of the poor. Proverbs 19:17 (NIV) states, _Whoever is kind to the poor lends to the Lord, and he will reward them for what they have done._ Proverbs 11:24-25 (NIV) goes on to say, _One person gives freely, yet gains even more; another withholds unduly, but comes to poverty. A generous person will prosper; whoever refreshes others will be refreshed._ It's seems God knows the blessing received within a generous heart; it's part of the abundant life He came to give us (John 10:10)! Psalm 41:8 finds the enemy declaring defeat before the end of the game! The enemy likes to do that but don't let the enemy trick you!! The enemy thought they had won at the cross but the game wasn't over!! Three days later the enemy's eyes probably popped outta socket to see Jesus walk free and living out of the grave!!! *Micah 7:8 (NIV) Do not gloat over me, my enemy! Though I have fallen, I will rise. Though I sit in darkness, the LORD will be my light.* Psalm 41:9 speaks of betrayal by a close friend. Jesus also experienced the betrayal of a close friend - Judas (See Matthew 26:17-30 also John 13:18). *For we do not have a high priest who is unable to empathize with our weakness, but we have one who has been tempted in every way, just as we are - yet he did not sin. Hebrews 4:15 (NIV)*

- Book 2 of the Psalms includes Psalms 42-72. Psalm 41 is by the Levitical choir appointed by David. It's interesting that it is the descendants of Korah who wrote this Psalm. Korah was the one who had rebelled against Moses and ended up getting his whole family swallowed up by the earth (see Numbers 16:1-50)! And yet somehow, someway hope survived! Hope place in Jesus will never disappoint! Just as this Psalm continues to declare their steadfast placement of hope in God whose love is unfailing (the Korah-ites of all people should know right!) Psalm 42 begins with a thirstiness of the soul and a feast of tears. Isaiah 55 extends an invite to the thirsty. In just the first verse of Isaiah 55 (NIV) it's stated, *"Come, all you who are thirsty, come to the waters; and you who have no money, come, buy and eat! … verse 2 … Listen, listen to me, and eat what is good, and you will delight in the richest of fare.* In John 4:34 Jesus speaks of uncommon food. His disciples come back with food for Him after He has revealed Who He is to the samaritan woman at the well and they say… *"Rabbi, eat something." But he said to them, "I have food to eat that you know nothing about."* John 4:31-32 (NIV) and in verse 34 Jesus explains, *"My food," said Jesus, "is to do the will of him who sent me and to finish his work.* When hope seems lost remember things are not always as they seem just as Isaiah 55:8-9 reminds us. So take control in the areas Scripture says we can, like in 2 Corinthians 10:5 (NIV) …*take captive every thought to make it obedient to Christ.* And put your mind on Truth… *being confident of this, that he who began a good work in you will carry it on to completion until the day of Christ Jesus. Philippians 1:6 (NIV)*

- *Psalm 43:3 (NLT) Send out your light and your truth; let them guide me.* Jesus says in *John 12:46 (NIV) I have come into the world as a light, so that no one who believes in me should stay in darkness.* Choose to remain in Truth, the Word (Scriptures) and you will always find the Living Word (Jesus Christ), and you will have the Light of life (John 8:12, John 14:6)!

- Psalm 44:22 is found quoted in Romans 8:36. Please take a moment and see the context this verse is contained in as you read Romans 8:18-39 (especially verses 31-39). So back to Psalm 44 and frame their confusion (much like our own when we see the seemingly good or innocent suffer) with the Truth of Romans 8. It doesn't make it easy but the light of our hope has not been snuffed out! Suffering does not indicate a lack of love for the

Father loves the Son and gave Him up to save us all (Romans 8:32). Isaiah 53 describes the sacrifice of Jesus and in verses 11-12 (NLT) it is recorded, *When he sees all that is accomplished by his anguish he will be satisfied. And because of his experience, my righteous servant will make it possible for many to be counted righteous, for he will bear all their sins. I will give him the honors of a victorious soldier...* There is purpose for the pain and reward for enduring faithfully. *For now we see only a reflection as in a mirror; then we shall see face to face. Now I know in part; then I shall know fully, even as I am fully known. 1 Corinthians 13:12 (NIV)* In all you do not know, all of you, is all known by Him. He has not lost track of one part, even in all the parts that seem lost to you. *Though he slay me, yet will I hope in him; ... Job 13:15 (NIV)*

• Psalm 45 is considered one of the Messianic Psalms as it portrays our Messiah. For example Psalm 45:6-8 is fulfilled in Jesus Christ (see Hebrews 1:8-9). We can also find the wedding picture in Psalm 45:13-17 ultimately fulfilled in Revelation 19:6-8 and 21:2, between the Lamb of God and the bride, who is the church! Our God is faithful yesterday, today and forever (Hebrews 13:8)! He is who He claims to be in the Scriptures and He will do what He says He will do! Amen! Place your hope on the Rock through your trust in His Word and we will not be shaken. *Though the mountains be shaken and the hills be removed, yet my unfailing love for you will not be shaken nor my covenant of peace be removed," says the LORD, who has compassion you. Isaiah 54:10 (NIV)*

"Cool Down": The coolest thing revealed to you today was…

_____

_____

_____

_____

_____

_____

_____

God bless you muchly my cool friend~

~ DAY 10 ~

Date: _____

You thrill me, LORD, with all you have done for me! I sing for joy because of what you have done. Psalm 92:4 (NLT) What a gift to be alive today! A heartbeat is a gift only God Almighty can give and He only does things with great plan and purpose. So rejoice that He wants YOU apart of His day! (And I do too! So thank you for joining me today, let's begin!!)

Warm Up and Worship:

_____

_____

Pray Scripture: *Search me, God and know my heart; test me and know my anxious thoughts. See if there is any offensive way in me, and lead me in the way everlasting. Psalm 139:23-24 (NIV)* Please continue in prayer with God as you open your time with Him in the lead.

P.R. & P.R.

_____

_____

_____

_____

_____

_____

_____

_____

_____

_____

Daily Devotional Reading: "Un-fragile Joy"

Those the LORD has rescued will return. They will enter Zion with singing; everlasting joy will crown their heads. Gladness and joy will overtake them, and sorrow and sighing will flee away. Isaiah 51:11 (NIV)

True joy runs deeper than mere happiness; it just comes thicker. True joy cannot be penetrated by situations that surround you. Joy supersedes the fragility of happiness. This un-fragile joy is freely open for the embracing yet hinges on two things: Where you place your hope and how you understand the love of Jesus.

Jesus Christ holds up under any expectation. *We have this hope as an anchor for the soul, firm and secure. … Hebrews 6:19 (NIV)* Jesus entered this imperfect world, into an imperfect family, during imperfect political times. He chose to do this so that among all the imperfect things that tempt our grasp for security and fulfillment He Himself could be that one perfect Living Hope; that soul filling joy of salvation!

Jesus' love is stronger than the worst of me/you. To understand that fact, to truly believe God's love for you is unconditional becomes a game changer. Trust grows in a love filled relationship and hope can be placed in what we can trust. It is imperative that we hinge our hope on Jesus and frame your understanding of His love by His trustworthy Word and we will find our souls flooded with unshatterable joy dear one!

This joy in Jesus, as depicted in Scripture cannot be shattered by shattering life circumstances. See Acts 5 when the apostles are persecuted, beaten and yet emerge rejoicing! Not because the experience was happy but rather their hope was hinged on a God of eternal good news! Good news that there is a better day coming because Jesus loved us enough to enter into our imperfection and overcame by His sacrifice in our place on the cross, rising again on the third day!! Now we too, like the apostles in Acts 5, can keep on *"day after day"* (Acts 5:42) in this joy that supersedes the fragile emotion of happiness! *They go from strength to strength, till each appears before God in Zion. Psalm 84:7 (NIV)*

Because of God's unfailing love for you and a sure hope of a better day coming in Jesus, you can embrace an unshatterable joy in and through all days, no matter what comes your way dear one! You are not alone (Matt. 28:10). *He will wipe every tear from their eyes. There will be no more death' or mourning or crying or pain, for the old order of things has passed away." Revelation 21:4 (NIV)* Praise God! For today there is joy in that we are just one more day closer to our God making all things new!!

Defeat the enemy of your happiness by choosing to embrace the joy in Jesus available today dear one. *Blessed is the one who perseveres under trial because, having stood the test, that person will receive the crown of life that the Lord has promised to those who love him. James 1:12 (NIV)*

"Remember not the former things, nor consider the things of old. Isaiah 43:18 (ESV) Behold, I am doing a new thing; now it springs forth, do you not perceive it? I will make a way in the wilderness and rivers in the desert. Isaiah 43:19 (ESV) And he who was seated on the throne said, "Behold, I am making all things new." Also he said, "Write this down, for these words are trustworthy and true." Revelation 21:5 (ESV) "For behold, I create new heavens and a new earth, and the former things shall not be remembered or come to mind. Isaiah 65:17 (ESV)

~~~

Study in the Psalms: Today we will be reading Psalms 46, 47, 48, 49 and 50.

- Converse with God as you read through each Psalm.
- Pause and reflect on verses that catch your heart's attention.
- Record one verse from each Psalm that holds impact for you.
- Review your list. Is there a theme in the verses you highlighted? Take time and listen for God's voice to your heart.

- My favorite verse from Psalm 46:

  _____

  _____

  _____

- My favorite verse from Psalm 47:

  _____

  _____

  _____

- My favorite verse from Psalm 48:

_____

_____

_____

- My favorite verse from Psalm 49:

_____

_____

_____

- My favorite verse from Psalm 50:

_____

_____

_____

Five additional points to ponder from our Scripture passages today. (I do hope, if nothing else, these bullet points each day encourage you in further research of His eternal Word.)

- Psalms 46-48 are praise hymns and probably written over victory in battle. Do we remember to praise God for our victories over our own battles… just as much as we pray for His help within them? Jerusalem was a city without a water source which was strange and made it vulnerable to an enemy. At one such a time Jerusalem was surrounded by an Assyrian enemy who thought they had a victory in the bag if only they could wait it out long enough for those in Jerusalem to get thirsty enough! However on to the enemy's scheme king Hezekiah had his men dig a tunnel from an outside spring so that water would flow straight into the city!

Covering up the outside source the enemy had no idea they had sustaining water flowing from within! (See 2 Kings 18-19, 2 Chronicles 32:30) Psalm 46:5 (NIV) one of my all time favorite verses states, *God is within her, she will not fall; God will help her at break of day.* We too as believers in Jesus have sustaining strength within that will help us outwit the enemy of our lives too! John 7:37 (NIV) … *Jesus stood and said in a loud voice, "Let anyone who is thirsty come to me and drink. Whoever believes in me, as Scripture has said, rivers of living water will flow from within them."* 2 Corinthians 2:11 reminds us we are not unaware of the enemy's schemes so do not let him outwit you!! *2 Corinthians 4:7 (NIV) But we have this treasure in jars of clay to show that this all-surpassing power is from God and not from us. Colossians 1:27 (NLT) For God wanted them to know that the riches and glory of Christ are for you Gentiles, too. And this is the secret: Christ lives in you. This gives you assurance for sharing his glory.* Psalm 46:10 beckons us to just stand still before Him. If we will be still in Him, reverence just Who our Almighty God of Heavens Armies is, Who He is to us, that He loves you - unfailingly… we can stand without falling before anyone or within any situation dear one. Psalm 46:2-3 (NIV) *Therefore we will not fear,* (why?, because it's not the spirit He's given us! See 2 Timothy 1:7 (parenthesis mine)) *though the earth give way and the mountains fall into the heart of the sea, though its waters roar and foam and the mountains quake with their surging.* Sounds like a pretty fearful scenario and yet we can, in Christ, look to the cross and the empty tomb and know we have nothing to fear! We will be brought through safely to His Heavenly Kingdom for eternity in the end or shall I say, in just the beginning (2

Timothy 4:18)!!!! As in the book of Job, when God allows the waters of our world to rage it's to bring us closer to His heart, to reveal a depth of His character we never would have known otherwise; it's for our ultimate good and His glory (see Romans 8:28). In all Job experienced, in all he couldn't understand and through all he was asked to endure… the last chapter of Job reveals not a falling away from the faith but rather a strengthening of trust through greater revelations of God. Job chose to believe God faithful even if, even when, even though… and God was. He drew near in the tears. *Job 42:5 (NIV) My ears had heard of you but now my eyes have see you. John 16:20 (NIV) … You will grieve, but your grief will turn to joy.*

- Psalm 47:7 declares God to be King over all the earth and in verse 8, reigning over the nations. With that Truth He surely has my situation and circumstance covered! I am free to praise His faithfulness to me in the past with expectation for Him to be consistently faithful presently and forever! His way's will always be best so my best bet is to surrender my illusion of control and allow Him to work His will on earth in my life as it is in Heaven (Matthew 6:10). Psalm 47:1 instructs us to clap and to shout in praise of our God… that to me means obey in word AND action. Wholehearted devotion combats the double mindedness that always leads to being tossed about on the wind and waves of doubt. *Do not conform to the pattern of this world, but be transformed by the renewing of your mind. Then you will be able to test and approve what God's will is - his good, pleasing and perfect will. Romans 12:2 (NIV)*

- Psalm 48 ends with a wonderful reminder (verse 14) that our God will stand with us forever and guide us all the way Home. We have His faithful and trustworthy Word as our map and the Holy Spirit as our Guide. If we will take Him up on His offer, walking humbly with Him (Micah 6:8) we will not ever be lost. Verse 13 reminds us to remember His faithfulness and tell of Him to the next generation! How are you reminding yourself of His faithfulness? How are your spiritual eyes being kept alert? How are you being given opportunity to influence the next generation? Are we using those opportunities - trusting God with our effectiveness? *Pray for us, too, that God will give us many opportunities to speak about his mysterious plan concerning Christ. … verse 4, Pray that I will proclaim this message as clearly as I should. Colossians 4:3-4 (NIV)* Psalm 48:9 reminds us to think on God's unfailing love. How would this change your perspective of your situation, life, relationships… if your thought life was wrapped up in God's unfailing love for you?! See Philippians 4:8. *Psalm 63:3 (NIV) Because your love is better than life, my lips will glorify you.*

- *Psalm 49:15 (NLT) But as for me, God will redeem my life. He will snatch me from the power of the grave.* Salvation cannot be bought or earned. *For as you know that it was not with perishable things such as silver or gold that you were redeemed from the empty way of life handed down to you from your ancestors, but with the precious blood of Christ, a lamb without blemish or defect. 1 Peter 1:18-19 (NIV)* See also Hebrews 9:11-15, Mark 10:45. *In him we have redemption through his blood, the forgiveness of sins, in accordance with the riches of God's grace Ephesians 1:7 (NIV) For God so loved the world that he gave his one and only Son, that whoever believes in him shall not perish but have eternal life. John 3:16 (NIV) Psalm 49:17 (NIV) for they will take nothing with them when they die, their splendor will not descend with them.* We cannot take our wealth with us but we can in a sense, send it on ahead, *"Do not store up for yourselves treasures on earth, where moths and vermin destroy, and where thieves break in and steal. But store up for yourselves treasures in heaven, where moths and vermin do not destroy, and where thieves do not break in and steal. For where your treasure is, there you heart will be also. Matthew 6:19-21 (NIV)* Love God, love people (Matthew 22:37-40) *By this everyone will know that you are my disciples, if you love one another." Join 13:35 (NIV)* We were made to be a display of HIS splendor! Dear one, root down into Him and He will grow you up in such a way that… *They will be called oaks of righteousness, a planting of the Lord for the display of his splendor. Isaiah 61:3 (NIV)* His splendor is the only splendor that matters and He will make you a beautiful reflection of Himself as you display the treasure of Him within through love (Romans 5:5). A mighty oak was once just a sapling that refused to give up. Keep growing up into Him rather than on the ladder this world deems as success dear one. The only way truly up, is down into Him.

- Psalm 50 issues a warning for willful wickedness and hypocritical love. *Yet a time is coming and has now come when the true worshipers will worship the Father in the Spirit and in truth, for they are the kind of worshipers the Father seeks. John 4:23 (NIV)* Psalm 50:14 (NLT) states, *Make thankfulness your sacrifice to God,* …. Sometimes thankfulness is a sacrifice but when we trust God, when we choose to take Him at

His faithful Word to know the plans, good plans (Jeremiah 29:11) and that He indeed is working all things, ALL things for good (Romans 8:28) we can choose a spirit of praise, of gratitude, for our God is our Warrior through worship (see 2 Chronicles 20)! *Rejoice in the Lord always. … Philippians 4:4 (NIV)* We can always rejoice IN the Lord for He alone saves. *Trust in him at all times, you people; pour out your hearts to him, for God is our refuge. Psalm 62:8 (NIV)* Psalm 50 ends with this in verse 23 (NLT)*, But giving thanks is a sacrifice that truly honors me…* When we submit our will and way offering a sacrifice of thanks He will delight our hearts with what delights His. What more could we desire than to be a delight to HIS heart!! *Now that you have purified yourselves by obeying the truth so that you have sincere love for each other, love one another deeply, from the heart. 1 Peter 1:22 (NIV)* We can only love sincerely when we are sincerely connected to Love Himself (1 John 4:8). After all we owe all to Him, *And who has given him so much that he needs to pay it back? Romans 11:35 (NLT)* We owe our very heartbeat, the fact we woke up this morning to Him. May we worship Him in sincerity and truth, humbly offering a sacrifice of praise through all our days.

"Cool Down":

_____

_____

_____

_____

_____

_____

_____

Thank you for meeting me here! As I look out my window it is blizzard like conditions and I'm grateful that "God's gym" His Word is ever available to us, open to us rain or shine! Our hearts can flourish (even in a blizzard) especially when we commit His Word to memory and hide it in our hearts. God bless you muchly~

... But God's word is not chained. 2 Timothy 2:9 (NIV)

~ DAY 11 ~

Date: _____

Welcome I'm so glad to see you've made it back! I appreciate your perseverance. No one wants to be caught spiritually sleeping and your tenacity to continue diligently carving out time to saturate in Truth is inspiring! We can't complete the race marked out for us if we aren't up and "running" right! Which reminds me of Matthew 26. Just before Jesus went to the cross He went to the garden to pray. He brought three disciples with Him and every time He checked they had fallen back to sleep! Matthew 26:40-41 (NIV) reads like this, *Then he returned to his disciples and found them sleeping. "Couldn't you men keep watch with me for one hour?" He asked Peter. "Watch and pray so that you will not fall into temptation. The spirit is willing, but the flesh is weak."* We know the enemy is out there prowling around looking for someone to devour (1 Peter 5:8) and though the exact temptation is not named in Matthew 26, Jesus just advices praying before we even face it. Jesus advices us again on this when teaching us how to pray in Matthew 6. He says, *And lead us not into temptation, but deliver us from the evil one.' Matthew 6:13 (NIV)* Seems such a prayer to pray against temptation before we are even aware of what it may be, is wise. It is wise and requires spiritual alertness. Jesus knew in this world we would be up against a great enemy and all kinds of hardship but nothing His victory wouldn't or hasn't trumped. *"I have told you these things, so that in me you may have peace. In this world you will have trouble. But take heart! I have overcome the world." John 16:33 (NIV)* Jesus goes on in John chapter 17 to pray for us! As I was reading through that chapter this morning I was touched specifically by verse 17. You see, right now one of my daughters is taking a High School History class. Our children attend secular school and I know God calls every individual to different places at different times, however for us, at this time, as we have laid it before God, we feel we are to be in the secular arena. With that also comes secular curriculum. We try to use the moments that the curriculum would go against Truth to embolden our children's faith to know what they believe and not be afraid to stand on it. This particular morning my daughter was telling me she had a quiz coming up on evolution. Only God would have foreseen this conversation and had my early morning reading direct me specifically to John 17! The chapter in which Jesus knew it would be hard to live in this world and not be of it so He prays specifically over His own! I was able to claim Jesus' prayer for all of us in John 17 as my prayer specifically tailored to my current life situation with my kids in secular school and specifically over my daughter as she faces that class daily in doctrine we know is not Truth. *Sanctify them by the truth; your word is truth. John 17:17 (NIV)* How did Jesus handle knowing we would be left in this world amongst an enemy prowling around to devour us?! He taught Truth, lived out Truth and He prayed. How do we handle letting go of our children, those we love, into a world that is harsh? We teach Truth, live out Truth and we pray. Pray for one another to not fall to the enemies schemes but to be fearlessly set apart in heart and mind by His Truthful Word.

Warm Up and Worship:

_____

_____

Pray Scripture: *Therefore, get rid of all moral filth and the evil that is so prevalent and humbly accept the word planted in you, which can save you. James 1:21 (NIV)* Dear Heavenly Father You have given us Truth! Thank You! Keep us spiritually awake and may we ever be captivated by Your trustworthy heart above all else. In Jesus name. Please continue praying to begin your time with God.

P.R. & P.R.

_____

_____

_____

_____

_____

_____

_____

_____

_____

Daily Devotional Reading: "The Fruitfulness Of Forgetfulness"

Joseph named his firstborn Manasseh and said, "it is because God has made me forget all my trouble and all my father's household." The second son he named Ephraim and said, "It is because God has made me fruitful in the land of my suffering." Genesis 41:51-52 (NIV)

Forgetting the fudges of the past produces present and future fruitfulness in one's life. If we cannot forgive AND forget, our roots become bitter and rot out our purpose on this planet. How do we truly forget all the hurts and the wrongs done to us, we all wonder?! That's impossible!! And yet… *Matthew 19:26 (NLT) Jesus looked at them intently and said, "Humanly speaking, it is impossible. But with God everything is possible."* So maybe selective memory IS possible, BUT if God has allowed the memories to remain then there is good that can come through them (Romans 8:28).

If we never remembered a wrong done to us we would never know personally the emotional cost of forgiveness. We would then lose out on the dynamic dimension of God's deep love revealed to us as we remember how short we have fallen and yet stand forgiven and justified through faith in Christ! *For all have sinned and fall short of the glory of God, Romans 3:23 (NIV) But God demonstrates his own love for us in this: while we were still sinners, Christ died for us. Romans 5:8 (NIV) If you declare with your mouth, "Jesus is Lord," and believe in your heart that God raised him from the dead, you will be saved. Romans 10:9 (NIV) Therefore, there is now no condemnation for those who are in Christ Jesus, Romans 8:1 (NIV)*

Even when we cannot forget with our mind we can choose not to harbor any record of the wrongs in our hearts. *1 Corinthians 13:4-5 (NIV) Love is patient, love is kind. It does not envy, it does not boast, it is not proud. It does not dishonor others, it is not self-seeking, it is not easily angered, it keeps no record of wrongs.*

We can choose never to mention it again with our tongues. *Proverbs 18:21 (NIV) The tongue has the power of life and death, and those who love it will eat its fruit.*

At times when our thoughts tempt us back we can choose rather to take captive those thoughts and make them again obedient to Christ. *2 Corinthians 10:5 (NIV) We demolish arguments and every pretension that sets itself up against the knowledge of God, and we take captive every thought to make it obedient to Christ.* We can choose to re-fix our focus, re-fix our gaze - *fixing our eyes on Jesus, the pioneer and perfecter of faith. For the joy set before him he endured the cross, scorning its shame, and sat down at the right hand of the throne of God. Hebrews 12:2 (NIV) Finally, brothers and sisters, whatever is true, whatever is noble, whatever is right, whatever is pure, whatever is lovely, whatever is admirable- if anything is excellent or praiseworthy- think about such things. Philippians 4:8 (NIV)*

Our God is fully qualified to handle our past, we have enough to bear facing forward in faith and by His grace may what we bear be fruitful. *Do not seek revenge or bear a grudge against anyone among your people, but love your neighbor as yourself. I am the Lord. Leviticus 19:18 (NIV)* Our Heavenly Father is worthy of the fruit our lives would produce through our willingness to forgive and forget.

Today may your life be dripping with sweet juicy goodness that only comes from the freeing fruit of forgiving forgetfulness dear one, and may you be able to declare, ...*God has made me fruitful in the land of my suffering.*" *Genesis 41:52 (NIV)*

~~~

Study in the Psalms: Today we will be reading Psalms 51, 52, 53, 54 and 55.

- Converse with God as you read through each Psalm.
- Pause and reflect on verses that catch your heart's attention.
- Record one verse from each Psalm that holds impact for you.
- Review your list. Is there a theme in the verses you highlighted? Take time and listen for God's voice to your heart.

- My favorite verse from Psalm 51:

_____

_____

_____

- My favorite verse from Psalm 52:

_____

_____

_____

- My favorite verse from Psalm 53:

  _____

  _____

  _____

- My favorite verse from Psalm 54:

  _____

  _____

  _____

- My favorite verse from Psalm 55:

  _____

  _____

  _____

Five additional points to ponder from our Scripture passages today after reading Psalms 51-55.

- Psalm 51 is David's prayer of confession and repentance after committing adultery with Bathsheba (See 2 Samuel 11:1-12:25). God died to save us from sin, so why are we so drawn to entertaining aspects of it in our lives? Sin - big or small, God died for it all! All sin cost God His Son's life! God knows sin is rotten to the core and will end up ultimately destroying us (rotting us to our core) and hurting those around us. Just look at David's affair with Bathsheba…what seemed pleasurable and enticing at first, ended up with a man murdered, a baby dying, a marriage destroyed and there was such great grief in every heart! God gave His life to keep us from such a pit and yet even still when we find ourselves there, He is gracious and merciful to pull us out when we cry out to Him. *He lifted me out of the slimy pit, out of the mud and mire; he set my feet on a rock and gave me a firm place to stand. Psalm 40:2 (NIV)* Psalm 51:10-12 is another one of my favorite Scripture passages to turn into a personal prayer. I also find verse 13 to prove David's trust in God's character, to faithfully move forward in God's purpose for him past the pain and regret of his failings. Jesus proves that He does have purpose and plans for us past our problems with past sins in John 21. After Peter denies even knowing Him as He is facing the cross (Not once or twice but three times!) Jesus comes back to make sure Peter knows he is still wanted on the mission field of life! John 21:15 (NIV) finds Jesus asking Peter a question. … *"Simon son of John, do you love me more than these?" "Yes, Lord,"* he said, *"you know that I love you." Jesus said, "Feed my lambs."* "Do you love Me more than these?" More than "these"… these insecurities, these regrets, these past failures, these rumors, these… you fill in the blank. What would keep you from forgiving what God has already forgiven if you have confessed and repented of it? What would keep you from stepping back up to the plate and trying again? Jesus clearly wants Peter back out to minister to the people. Isn't it where we have fallen and chosen to rest in the Truth of the cross, receiving forgiveness and new life by the power of His resurrection, that we have our best and most powerful ministry to others of the grace and mercy of our Savior?! Might it be so hard to overcome "these" what ever "these" defines for you because the enemy knows too, how powerful your ministry would be for God's Kingdom if you let your love of Jesus trump all "these" other things that are holding you back?! Oh dear one there is so much more to mine from this Psalm however we have 4 more to read today so we must move forward! But before we do let's tuck one more Truth into our hearts pocket. *If we confess our sins, he is faithful and just and will forgive us our sins and purify us from all unrighteousness. 1 John 1:9 (NIV)* Okay maybe one more will fit in that hearts pocket if we stuff right?! *For as high as the heavens are above the earth, so great is his love for those two fear him; as far as the east is from the west, so far has he removed our transgression from us. Psalm 103:11-12 (NIV)* Take Him at His Word and trek forward in faith!

- Psalm 52 reminds me that efficient does not always equal effective. The first four verses of this Psalm remind me that I can be really good at something that is really bad. Remember back to Psalm 19 verse 14 (NIV), *May these words of my mouth and this meditation of my heart be pleasing in your sight, LORD, my Rock and my Redeemer.* The meditation of my heart is something no one else can see or know but me... and of course God who knows and sees all. *Hebrews 4:13 (NIV) Nothing in all creation is hidden from God's sight. Everything is uncovered and laid bare before the eyes of him to whom we must give account.* Jesus is the Living Word and I need to consistently measure the murmurings, the whispers of my heart up against His Word. Because even in the deepest depths of me, I want what only He can see to make Him smile. I want to be like that olive tree David talks about in Psalm 52:8, flourishing in the House of God! Amen!

- Psalm 53 brings me back to Jesus' prayer in John 17 that we discussed a bit in the beginning go today's study. The world is going to combat Truth in it's own corruption but as Psalm 53:1 (NIV) declares, *The fool says in his heart, "There is no God." … Mark 3:29 (NIV) but whoever blasphemes against the Holy Spirit will never be forgiven; they are guilty of an eternal sin."* The one unforgivable sin is to reject the One who can save you! How foolish! The Bible says we are all sinners, we see it here in Psalm 53, Psalm 14:2-3 and in Romans 3:10… if nothing else this information helps us extend a bit more grace in everyones direction right! See Romans 7:4-8:1. God is not effected by what we think of Him, we however, are eternally effected by what He thinks of us. Though we are all loved by God He honors our choice to love His Son Jesus as our Savior or not. *Jesus answered, "I am the way and the truth and the life. No one comes to the Father except through me. John 14:6 (NIV)* EVERYONE has the invitation. An invitation requires an RSVP. Through believing in Jesus Christ as the Scriptures say, we respond having accepted the invite and the door to eternity is swung wide open! *The fear of the LORD is the beginning of knowledge, but fools despise wisdom and instruction. Proverbs 1:7 (NIV)* A person can have 5 doctor degrees and yet without the reverent holy fear of God that person really knows nothing at all for the fear of the Lord is the BEGINNING of knowledge! *1 Corinthians 1:25-29 (NIV) For the foolishness of God is wiser than human wisdom, and the weakness of God is stronger than human strength. Brothers and sisters, think of what you were when you were called. Not many of you were wise by human standards; not many were influential; not many were of noble birth. But God chose the foolish things of the world to shame the wise; God chose the weak things of the world to shame the strong. God chose the lowly things of this world and the despised things- and the things that are not to nullify the things that are, so that no one may boast before him.* 2 Peter 3:9-10 (NIV) affords us all a warning worth heeding. *The Lord is not slow in keeping his promise, as some understand slowness. Instead he is patient with you, not wanting anyone to perish, but everyone to come to repentance. But the day of the Lord will come like a thief. The heavens will disappear with a roar; the elements will be destroyed by fire, and the earth and everything done in it will be laid bare.* As we embark on our next Psalm let's first savor 2 Corinthians 6:2 (NIV) for there is no time like the present to make a good choice. *For he says, "In the time of my favor I heard you, and in the day of salvation I helped you." I tell you, now is the time of God's favor, now is the day of salvation.*

• Psalm 54:6 speaks of a freewill offering or a voluntary offering. Isn't this the kind of gift we all like best to receive?! One not forced. *2 Corinthians 9:7 (NIV) Each of you should give what you have decided in your heart to give, not reluctantly of under compulsion, for God loves a cheerful giver.* Psalm 54:4-5 combines praise to prayer and we can pray in that same way! Praises and prayers combined! In just 7 short verses David goes from "Save me!" to "I have triumphed!". We are all to walk by faith and not sight but faith is anything but blind! Faith actually sees MORE! Faith takes God's Word, the beauty of His promises and sees forward to His glory from within the gloom! Thus God's child can have a peace that passes understanding and a hope that does not disappoint, at all times (Philippians 4:7, Romans 5:5)!

- *Psalm 55:22 (NIV) Cast your cares on the LORD and he will sustain you; he will never let the righteous be shaken.* We have this Truth to stand firm on even when our mood doesn't match our mission and we want to run away to the desert like David in Psalm 55:7! Who wants to run away and stay in the desert?! But sometimes in the hard times we can't think or see clearly and thus our judgment is also off! Like flying a plane; a pilot must fly by his instruments or crash because he can't see fully out the cockpit window! We, with finite minds and vision must navigate life with the instrument (His eternal Word) given to us by God who loves us and has good plans for us and sees all and understands all with His infinite mind! It's the only way we won't crash! *Psalm 55:16-18 (NIV) As for me, I call to God, and the LORD saves me. Evening, morning, and noon I cry out in distress, and he hears my voice. He rescues me unharmed from the battle waged against me, even though many oppose me.* Evening, morning, noon… that's a totally consumed focus. He hears, He saves, He rescues even though the odds are strong against me… that's fixed confidence. *Jeremiah 17:7-8 (NIV) "But blessed the one who trusts in the Lord, whose confidence is in him. They will be like a tree planted by the water that sends out its roots by the stream. It does not fear when heat comes; its leaves are always green. It has no worries in a year of drought and never fails to bear fruit."* Sounds like, in Jesus, we can thrive even if we are in a "desert". Much of Psalm 55 speaks of betrayal and Jesus also knows every bit how it feels to be betrayed! Jesus continually entrusted Himself into the Father's care just as we are too do (see Luke 23:46 and Isaiah 53:10-12) and received reward. *John 15:20 (NIV) Remember what I told you: 'A servant is not greater than his master.'*

If they persecuted me, they will persecute you also. … 2 Timothy 1:12 (NIV) That is why I am suffering as I am. Yet this is no cause for shame, because I know whom I have believed, and am convinced that he is able to guard what I have entrusted to him until that day. Come what may this side of Heaven, you are never alone (Hebrews 13:5); trust the strength of the Hand that sustains you. *…But as for me, I trust in you. Psalm 55:22 (NIV)*

"Cool Down": *'Call to me and I will answer you and tell you great and unsearchable things you do not know.' Jeremiah 33:3 (NIV)* Record the coolest thing God revealed to you today that you did not know before.

_____

_____

_____

_____

_____

_____

_____

God bless you for staying spiritually awake dear one!!

~ DAY 12 ~

Date: _____

Hello my dear friend. This morning I was shoveling the snow off our driveway which, actually I usually really enjoy. It's like vacuuming lines in your carpet… there is a small satisfaction that comes with completing a neatly patterned shoveled walk. (I don't know, am I letting my freak flag fly a bit too high?!) Well anyway, shoveling snow is usually just enough of a work out to get the blood pumping and the praise flowing. I say usually because once in a while we have a dumping so deep and heavy I'm way past blood pumping and into heart throb sweating, all winter gear is being hurled off with each hack at the avalanche of snow (no neat patterns on those days) we are forging a pathway out for mere survival folks! We have six kids we need the staples… milk, eggs, chocolate… In life (like the weather) we have the eb and flow of trials in their varying degrees too. Often in the Psalms we see the honest struggles of life and yet so often the closing of the hymn is with praise and hope! My prayer for us both is to endure every trail, no matter the size, with praise and hope because in the end, our God has won! Bottom line: we have the victory in our victorious God! Amen!

Warm Up and Worship:

_____

_____

Pray Scripture: *My heart, O God, is steadfast, my heart is steadfast; I will sing and make music. Psalm 57:7 (NIV)* Dear Heavenly Father fix our hearts, make them steadfast in You as we saturate in the Living Water of Your Word. Make our lives produce music that makes You smile, that makes You sing! *The LORD your God is in your midst, a mighty one who will save; he will rejoice over you with gladness; he will quiet you by his love; he will exult over you with loud singing. Zephaniah 3:17 (ESV)* Please continue in a time of prayer before proceeding.

P.R. & P.R.

_____

_____

_____

_____

_____

_____

_____

_____

_____

_____

_____

Daily Devotional Reading: "Use The Pressure To Press In"

If you fail under pressure, your strength is too small. Proverbs 24:10 (NLT)

If you have ever felt like you've failed under pressure, reading this Proverb makes one want to cry out, "Well then how do I get more strength?!" However I think the more effective cry of our hearts is, "How do I start using the strength I actually already have?!" In Christ it's not that you have too little strength but that we utilize too little of what we have! 1 John 4:4 reminds us that although we are little, great is the strength within us. *Little children, you are from God and have overcome them, for he who is in you is greater than he who is in the world.* (ESV)

Times of pressure are for our benefit in that it reveals to the wise where to take more ground in emotional self-control within the True promises of God (2 Tim. 1:7). The great prophet Jeremiah was honest about his struggles with the pressure of his calling and God was honest back about how to handle it. Jeremiah knew where to press in when the pressure heated up. Do we?!

In Jeremiah 12:5 God reminds him it's not going to get easier on this side of heaven. We must let the trial train us to turn in total dependence upon our Source of all, the great I Am (Ex. 3:14). In Jeremiah 15:19-21 (NLT) God says, ...*You must influence them; do not let them influence you! They will fight against you like an attacking army, but I will make you as secure as a fortified wall of bronze. They will not conquer you, for I am with you to protect and rescue you. I, the LORD, have spoken! Yes, I will certainly keep you safe from these wicked men. I will rescue you from their cruel hands.*"

So in this Truth we find that we will feel and see the effects of cruelty fighting against us like an attacking army. BUT we are not to let that influence us. Rather, we can rest our minds and hearts in the Truth that God will make us secure, strong and fortified, we will not be conquered but rescued and kept safely protected, we will not be overcome, for we battle IN our Conquering King (Jn. 16:33) and we have a Home not of this world. We are given these Truths to rest in but often the details of the strengthening, the rescuing, the fortifying... remain with Him. This strengthens our "dependence on Him" muscle, so that in our weakness, in our smallness, we become strong under pressure through trust.

He declares Himself to be the Word (John 1:1) so the way to increase our dependence on Him is to daily "dance" with Him in the Word. The more we know Him the more we can trust Him. Then, when under pressure we can press into the One we know and trust is above it all, and the Source of all the strength we need. *You, LORD, keep my lamp burning; my God turns my darkness into light.* Psalm 18:28 (NIV)

Where He calls, He leads.

- Noah, in the face of a trial that could literally have drowned him in fear, heard God call from out front, *"Come into the ark…* (Gen. 7:1 NKJV) God was already where He was calling Noah to go.

- The disciples wanted to know where to prepare the passover meal for Jesus and He sent them *…to a large room that is already set up.* (Mark 14:15 NLT)

You are not alone in what He is calling you to, *The LORD himself goes before you and will be with you; he will never leave you nor forsake you. Do not be afraid; do not be discouraged.* Deuteronomy 31:8 (NIV)

Dear overcomer (Rom. 8:37), when the pressure rises, don't let it make you think you have not what it takes; rather use it to press you into deeper dependence on the Source of your unending strength (2 Tim. 1:12).

~~~

Study in the Psalms: Today we will be reading Psalms 56, 57, 58, 59 and 60.

- Converse with God as you read through each Psalm.
- Pause and reflect on verses that catch your heart's attention.
- Record one verse from each Psalm that holds impact for you.
- Review your list. Is there a theme in the verses you highlighted? Take time and listen for God's voice to your heart.

- My favorite verse from Psalm 56:

_____

_____

_____

- My favorite verse from Psalm 57:

_____

_____

_____

- My favorite verse from Psalm 58:

_____

_____

_____

- My favorite verse from Psalm 59:

  _____

  _____

  _____

- My favorite verse from Psalm 60:

  _____

  _____

  _____

Five additional points to ponder.

- _Psalm 56:3 (NIV) when I am afraid, I put my trust in you._ What a wonderful verse to commit to memory. All those times we feel we don't know what to do, this verse reminds us just what to do! It is similar to another of my favorite memory verses; _2 Chronicles 20:12 (NIV) Our God, will you not judge them? For we have no power to face this vast army that is attacking us. We do not know what to do, but our eyes are on you."_ A verse is good to commit to memory because it jogs our heart to what is Truth, stabilizing us in times of turmoil; to bring about a triumph through a trouble. We can't have a triumph without a trial and this Psalm 56 is a model for how to continually frame your mindset on Truth. Go back to what you know is what my dad always says and Psalm 56:10 (NIV) finds David doing just that! _In God, whose word I praise, in the LORD, whose word I praise— verse 13-14, For you have delivered me from death and my feet from stumbling, that I may walk before God in the light of life._ When we go back to God's Word we are reminded that He already rescued us from eternal death AND He did so while we were still sinners NOT when we had our act together (Romans 5:8, 8:32)!!! So How much more having already done that will He not see you through everything else; for He who started a good work in you WILL carry it on to completion (Philippians 1:6)!! Dear one, you are loved, you are kept track of, even your tears are recorded (Psalm 56:8) along with the number of hairs on your head (Matthew 10:30)! Walk in the Light of Life! You can because He says you can and ALL authority has been given to Him and He is surely with you always (Matthew 28:18-20).

- Psalm 57 seems to have been through a night of fears to emerge with the dawn (verse 8) in victory!! His mercies are new every morning (Lamentations 3:22-23)! Psalm 57:1 finds David in trouble, hiding, but hiding in the right place! We can hide, turn inward in trouble, shut down inside the empty shell of self. Or we can turn outward, taking angry bitter revenge on the world around us, maybe even falling prey to a million other strongholds waiting to trap us further. OR we can turn upward to the God who holds ALL authority in His hand and let Him shelter us, reviving our souls through a saturation of Truth. Oh dear one, I'm praying you always turn upward! Pray Scripture with me, *Psalm 3:3 (NIV), But you, LORD, are a shield around me, my glory, the One who lifts my head high. Psalm 17:8 (NIV) Keep me as the apple of your eye; hide me in the shadow of your wings* - In Jesus victorious name, Amen. *John 10:28 (NIV) I give them eternal life, and they shall never perish; no one will snatch them out of my hand.* Praise Him who's arm is not to short to save

(Isaiah 59:1)!!

- Psalm 58 is one of the imprecatory Psalms that cry for justice so strongly that it almost sounds like a call for revenge. However we have a perfect and just Judge and He says, *Do not take revenge, my dear friends, but leave room for God's wrath, for it is written: "It is mine to avenge; I will repay," says the Lord. Romans 12:19 (NIV)* This Psalm provides opportunity for some good self evaluation. What are we doing with our sphere of influence? How are we handling the authority we have been given (we all have authority over something or someone)? James 2 reminds us not to show favoritism. *Listen, my dear brothers and sisters: Has not God chosen those who are poor in the eyes of the world to be rich in faith and to inherit the kingdom he promised those who love him? But you have dishonored the poor. Is it not he rich who are exploiting you? Are they not the ones who are dragging you into court? Are they not the ones who're blaspheming the noble name of him to whom you belong? James 2:5-7 (NIV)* Notice James' questions to us. The part that gets me is "But you have dishonored the poor. Is it not the rich who are exploiting you?" That would put me in the "poor" group too right…if I'm dishonoring the poor and the rich our exploiting me too! So even among our own people there is mistreatment, discord! It doesn't have to be so…a spoonful of humility always helps the rest of life go down a bit easier. *Romans 12:18 (NLT) Do all that you can to live in peace with everyone.* Are we really doing ALL that we can? Part of that effort is trusting God with what we cannot control and we cannot control others.

• Psalm 59:1 finds David asking for protection from his enemies and the prayer of John 17:17 comes to mind. Set me apart Lord, set me apart by Your Truth, Your Word is Truth! The best place to take refuge from the enemies piercing lies is within God's ironclad Truth. My NIV declares twice, in Psalm 59:10 and verse 17 that our God can be relied upon! In a fallible world this Truth is most comforting! Psalm 59:7 compares the enemies words to sharp swords. Whoever said, "sticks and stones will break my bones but words will never hurt" was oh so very wrong! *James 3:6 (NIV) The tongue also is a fire, a world of evil among the parts of the body. It corrupts the whole body, sets the whole corse of one's life on fire, and is itself set on fire by hell.* YIKES! *James 3:8 (NIV) but no human can tame the tongue. It is a restless evil, full of deadly poison.* Double YIKES!! Sounds like we all are susceptible to throwing darts, capable of hurling sharp swords in the form of poisonous deadly words that can kill self-esteem and annihilate relationships… we can all make the enemy's job easy when we do not submit our thoughts, words and actions to the Author of all authority. James 4:6 (NIV) reminds us, … *"God opposes the proud but shows favor to the humble."* If God opposes the proud, if pride puts distance between us and God, then what do you think the enemy will combat us with non-stop?! Every form of ugly pride there is and pride can come wrapped up beautifully! James 4:7 (NIV) gives us a way to combat the enemy's schemes, *Submit yourselves, then to God. Resist the devil, and he will flee from you.* In Jesus the enemy has no power over us, but we can give it to him. No human can tame the tongue but Jesus can. He will not take away what He died to give us, which is free will. Freedom is only truly found in Christ so let's choose not to quench His Spirit within us so that the only fire within us is that of His Word. May it be His life giving Word that God declares is like fire be what consumes us and is ever on our lips! May our words be life giving and used for building others up in His unfailing love. *But if I say, "I will not mention his word or speak anymore in his name," his word is in my heart like a fire, a fire shut up in my bones. I am weary of hold it in; indeed, I cannot. Jeremiah 20:9 (NIV)*

- *Psalm 60:12 (NIV) With God we will gain the victory, and he will trample down our enemies.* WITH GOD our victory is found. Apart from Him we can do NOTHING (John 15:5). With experience often grows confidence. No matter how old, or how experienced we become let us never, never forget that I AM (Exodus 3:14) is our everything. 2 Samuel 24 finds David at a point where he began to rely or look to his own strength only to fall mightily. It's easy if we are not fixed, heart, soul, mind and strength on Jesus, to get off course in this loud and distracting world. A world that offers "things" around every corner to tangibly place your trust in only to prove faulty, fluctuating and fallible. Pray Scripture with me, *Some trust in chariots and some in horses, but we trust in the name of the LORD our God. Psalm 20:7 (NIV) For in him all things were created: things in heaven and on earth, visible and invisible, whether thrones or powers or rulers or authorities; all things have been cerated through him and for him. He is before all things, and in him all things hold together. Colossians 1:16-17 (NIV)* Dear Heavenly Father please forgive us for when we have misplaced our trust, our allegiance. Please help us to place our trust not in "things" but rather in You who created all "things" and hold all "things" together, including us! You are our Victor and our only sure victory! Please grant us ever increasing child-like trust in You (Matthew 18:1-5). We thank and praise You!! In the matchless, merciful name of Jesus, Amen.

"Cool Down": What has made you feel fit to flourish in your faith today, through time in His Word?

_____

_____

_____

_____

_____

_____

_____

God bless you muchly~

~ DAY 13 ~

Date: _____

Welcome my fellow friend in the faith!

Warm Up and Worship: What will you choose to let your mind and heart marinate over in gratitude to warm up in worship today?

_____

_____

Pray Scripture: *May God be merciful and bless us. May his face smile with favor on us. Psalm 67:1 (NIV)* Please continue in prayer to prepare your mind and heart to receive Him.

P.R. & P.R.

_____

_____

_____

_____

_____

_____

_____

_____

_____

_____

Daily Devotional Reading: "What are you, mighty mountain?!"

So he said to me, "This is the word of the LORD to Zerubbabel: 'Not by might nor by power, but by my Spirit,' says the LORD Almighty. "What are you, mighty mountain? Before Zerubbable you will become level ground. Then he will bring out the capstone to shouts of 'God bless it! God bless it!'"
Zechariah 4:6-7 (NIV)

I live near a mighty mountain called Horsetooth. It appears to have a giant rock shaped tooth at the very top that is visible for miles! I have yet to climb it. I may or may not be afraid it will quite literally bite me! This might be because the majority of my climbing exercises are done on the stairs of my own home (and usually only when I need to go to bed at night)!

Over time I've learned that trying to contain the extent of our life experience to the flat land (where we can frame quite nicely the illusion of control) only makes the uncontrollable mountains seem mighty daunting overhead with pretty convincing threats to devour us alive!

Recalling the story of Peter walking on water amidst the wind and the waves with Jesus, found in Matthew 14, I'm reminded of who initiated the event. Jesus does call Peter out of the boat however it is Peter who asks Him to. Peter had the desire and drive in his heart to experience life in God to the full! He did not want to miss even one adventure God might be willing to take him on. So Peter in a sense flat out asks, "Take me out of this flat boat! Take me up on the mountainous waves with You Lord!" So Jesus calls Peter out on a word!!! "Come!" Jesus wants us all to embrace wave walking faith! He died to give us abundant life (that doesn't mean easy) just full of Who really matters.

How often do we let the big adventure float right by us just waiting for God to call us out when we haven't even asked Him to?! It's one thing to ask and have Him say "no". If He closes the door we better not knock it down, BUT maybe He'll say, "yes!" Like Peter, let's base our interpretation of what we hear on the firm foundation of God's Word.

What do you want bad enough to ask for it, unhindered by the fear of what He may answer? Peter could have wanted to walk on water but even still held back in asking because he was unable to rationalize past if Jesus said, "yes"! What if God says, "Come."? What then? I've never walked on water before, I'm so unqualified, so inexperienced... We can talk ourselves right out of conquering the mighty mountain before we even ask to get out of the boat to try! I wonder if there is a "what if..." you need to cast overboard so that you can float forward in faith and flourish like you were meant to in God?!

In Zechariah 4:6 Zerubbabel was reminded by God that his looming challenge would not be mastered by strength or power. See, this was important for Zerubbabel to be schooled in because he, in fact, did not have the royal power and might that both Solomon and David had. This feeling of inadequacy has kept how many of us from lending ourselves available to allow God to be our Ability in our avail-Ability?!

God reminds Zerubbable his mastery would come by way of His Holy Spirit! This Truth is followed by verse 7 in which God makes clear the "mighty mountain" will be leveled!

The size of your mountain, your impossibility, can be leveled by the size of your God, but will you ask? And if you ask, will you listen and respond in surrendered obedience, trusting He holds your best adventure? Dear one, take time with God, that you might confidently declare that whatever your mighty mountain is looming overhead, it certainly is no match for His mighty Holy Spirit within you!

If you, then, though you are evil, know how to give good gifts to your children, how much more will your Father in heaven give good gifts to those who ask him! Matthew 7:11 (NIV)

~ ~ ~

Study in the Psalms: Today we will be reading Psalms 61, 62, 63, 64 and 65.

- Converse with God as you read through each Psalm.
- Pause and reflect on verses that catch your heart's attention.
- Record one verse from each Psalm that holds impact for you.
- Review your list. Is there a theme in the verses you highlighted? Take time and listen for God's voice to your heart.

- My favorite verse from Psalm 61:

  _____

  _____

  _____

- My favorite verse from Psalm 62:

  _____

  _____

  _____

- My favorite verse from Psalm 63:

  _____

  _____

  _____

- My favorite verse from Psalm 64:

  _____

  _____

  _____

- My favorite verse from Psalm 65:

  _____

  _____

  _____

Five additional points to ponder.

- Psalm 61 is a prayer full of wonderful reminders of what prayer can be and do for us. Verse 2 says the psalmist is calling from the ends of the earth, so maybe he was far from home. However prayer is not hindered by geographical proximity. Our prayers can wrap up and around our loved ones even when we may be miles apart. Job states in *Job 23:9-10 (NIV) When he is at work in the north, I do not see him; when he turns to the south, I catch no glimpse of him. But he knows the way that I take; when he has tested me, I will come forth as gold.* Job was confident that even though he may have felt lost he was not lost from God's sight and care. Psalm 139:9-10 (NIV) also mirrors this confidence, *If I rise on the wings of the dawn, if I settle on the far side of the sea, even there your hand will guide me, your right hand will hold me fast.* So no matter where you are, remember feelings are often not facts and we can follow through on the promise in Hebrews 4:16 (NIV) from anywhere… geographically or emotionally. *Let us then approach God's throne of grace with confidence, so that we may receive mercy and find grace to help us in our time of need. John 16:24 (NIV) Until now you have not asked for anything in my name. Ask and you will receive, and your joy will be complete.* The more we commune with Him in the asking the more He can transform our perspective of what we really want; changing our asking if need be so that what we ultimately receive will be what makes our joy complete. Remember according to Ephesians 3:20 God is able to do immeasurably more than all we ask or imagine for it's in 1 Corinthians 2:9 that He tells us what He's doing for those who love Him is something no eye has seen, no ear has heard or what even any human mind has conceived!! Friends let's not miss communing with Him who holds joy complete; whether we feel near or far, high or low, He is always ready and waiting to meet! … lead me to the Rock that is higher than I!! (Psalm 61:2 NIV)

- Psalm 62 holds wonderful self talk. Verses 1 and 2 embolden his confidence as he heads into what troubles him in verses 3 and 4 but only to steady himself once more in verses 5 and 6 in what he knows is truth! Typically the thoughts that run through our heads eventually govern our actions. What we know in theory must be lived out and what better way to remind ourselves how to live than to speak back to ourselves what God has spoken to us in His Word! Don't give in to a spirit of fear that is not from God but rather live in the spirit He does give you that is full of power, love and a sound mind! A mind that can root on Truth and thus live walking forward in faith, unshaken (2 Timothy 1:7)! The two-faced personalities described in Psalm 62:4 is a warning extended to us all even in *1 John 4:20 (NIV) Whoever claims to love God yet hates a brother or sister is a liar. For whoever does not love their brother and sister, whom they have seen, cannot love God, whom they have not seen.* We want our lives to hold weight when it comes to the storms of life. We don't want to be a light-weight so to speak tossed on the wind and waves of doubt and fair-weather faithfulness. Psalm 62:9 reminded me of *Daniel 5:27 (NIV) Tekel: You have been weighed on the scales and found wanting.* YIKES! Psalm 62:10 reminds us where not to set our hearts… on the fleeting wealth of this world. *Proverbs 23:5 (NIV) Cast but a glance at riches, and they are gone, for they will surely sprout wings and fly off to the sky like an eagle.* Funny story… my husband and I were taking an evening walk one summer and our topic of conversation just happened to be about finances and wouldn't you know God brought His Word to life as He joined our conversation through the reminder of Proverbs 23:5 by sending and eagle soaring right over us just a arms length above almost!!! Straight down our neighborhood street!!! God sure knows how to get our attention and set our hearts on proper perspective! *And my God will meet all your needs according to the riches of his glory in Christ Jesus. Philippians 4:19 (NIV)* That's a good verse to commit to your self-talk list for sure!

- Psalm 63 finds David in the desert. We all go through "desert" seasons in life, times in the valley's. If we never had to go through the wilderness, if we only had mountain top high experiences we would never learn to walk by faith, only feelings. David sought God so earnestly that his longing consumed his senses! David thirsted for God, his whole being longed for Him Psalm 63:1 relays. Does our earnest seeking after God's heart consume our senses? Do we thirst for Him, look for Him, walk in ways to please Him, listen for Him, does what touches His heart touch ours in a way that moves our hands to become love, mercy and grace in action?! In the desert David remembers God's sanctuary and beholding His power and glory (verse 2). Do we take for granted the moments we are gifted to gather with other believers? *Hebrews 10:25 (NIV) not giving up meeting together, as some are in the habit of doing, but encouraging one another - and all the more as you see the Day approaching. 1 Thessalonians 5:9-11 (NIV) For God did not appoint us to suffer wrath but to receive salvation through our Lord Jesus Christ. He died for us so that, whether we are awake or asleep, we may live together with him. Therefore encourage one another and build each other up, just as in fact you are doing.* We all have choices in life, even in the desert seasons, and it would seem David continually chose to be animated with praise! Even in the night we can commune with Light Himself, we are never alone. Instead of counting sheep when we cannot sleep, like David in Psalm 63:6, we can think on our Shepherd! Count the ways of His faithfulness, either in your life or even within His Word. Pick a story from the Bible and just think on what it would have been like to be there at the rasing of Lazarus… what joy, what a thrill! *You thrill me, Lord, with all you have done for me! I sing for joy because of what you have done. Psalm 92:4 (NLT)* L.ife I.n G.od H.olds T.ruth remain in the Light to dispel the doubts in the dark.

- Psalm 64 speaks of the enemies attacks. The enemy is sure to attack that which is valuable to God so we must always be alert and on guard. Suit up with the armor of God (see Ephesians 6:10-18). Take up the sword of the Spirit which is the Word of God! The enemy will go after even that though so it's important we know Truth so well that the lies just look ridiculous. Jesus was able to untwist the enemy's lies in the desert because He knew Truth (Matthew 4). From the beginning the enemy has been attacking God's Word (see Genesis 3:1) because he knows how unstoppable we are if we believe Truth!! I'm reminded of Psalm 16 which we have already studied. Recall with me Psalm 16:5-6. The psalmist celebrates the boundary lines God has set. How often do we push the limits of those boundary lines (to the delight of the enemy)?! Never has an airplane pilot said, "let me see how little fuel I can put in my plane to get from point A to point B without having a crash landing." No! A pilot would not think to push those limits! Going on a flight they fuel up with as much as the plane will hold! No one plans to crash their life but how often do we fuel up in an effort to do all we can to live within the life giving bounds God has set for us in His Word? His boundaries afford the most abundant freedom in life (John 10:10)!! *Matthew 4:4 (NIV) Jesus answered, "It is written: 'Man shall not live on bread alone, but on every word that comes from the mouth of God.* The armor of God also includes the shield of faith that can extinguish all the flaming arrows of the evil one and Psalm 64:3 proves he is able to fire numerous arrows!! Interesting however that in Psalm 64:7 in the NKJV indicates God shoots back with AN arrow as in one! God doesn't need multiple arrows to defeat our enemies because God never misses. *But God shall shoot at them with an arrow; Suddenly they shall be wounded.* Raise your shield of faith, take up the sword of the Spirit, know Truth, live within the life giving boundaries God has set for your life and we too can know the rejoicing David speaks of in Psalm 64:10! David moved from fear in verse 1 to rejoicing by verse 10. We can enter into rejoicing regardless of how many flaming arrows are flying through our atmosphere when we remain living within the boundaries of God's Truth. P.S. If you are still breathing it's not to late to step back into those boundaries if you found you have strayed a step or two or even ten dear one.

- Psalm 65 is such an awesome Psalm of praise! Verse 8 states the whole earth is filled with awe at His wonders!! From the rising of the sun to its setting He inspires songs of joy!! All day long God is moving and inspiring within each one of His creatures and creations, songs of joy! The whole earth is filled with awe! Are you and I submitting to His inspirational filling?! 1 Thessalonians 5:19 reminds us God has given us control over how much of His filling we receive as He won't force our love and commitment. However He advises against us quenching His Spirit that He offers, for only in Him do we find full satisfaction, our inspired songs of joy dear one. Psalm 65 reminds us that He does answer prayer, He hears and forgives. Proverbs 28:9 (NIV) states, *If anyone turns a deaf ear to my instruction, even their prayers are detestable.* And tomorrow we will dive into Psalm 66 but a preview of verse 18 (NIV) also reveals similar information. *If I had cherished sin in my heart, the Lord would not have listened;* So our God does hear prayer but we must make sure when we pray we have cleaned out the connection lines by first confessing and repenting of any sin that would create distance between our Heavenly Father's heart and ours. Psalm 65 reminds us not to be fearful because He freely forgives all sincere repentance! I appreciate how this Psalm also pictures God's vast array of power. He is our hope, the One who formed the mountains, oh what might!! With that same mighty arm that He rose up the rocky mountains, He also extends out over the seas to still it to quiet gentleness. Then He turns and tends to the details of the land, caring for it, watering it, always aware of just what is needed. Interesting to me that as I have studied, I have misread the first two words of Psalm 65 repeatedly! In the NIV verse one begins, *Praise awaits…* and I have read it "Please wait!" I think God is trying to tell me something about patience maybe?! God answers prayer, His is our inspiration for all good ideas and songs of joy,

He is the only One who cares and tends to our details perfectly and has the ability to move our mountains or still us within as we climb them. He is always working from the rising of the sun to it's setting so maybe the key to receiving His inspired songs of joy is just to wait in Him, offering Him my simple availability to join Him in whatever, however, whenever, trusting that within that offer He will be my Ability - availAbility. *Praise awaits you, our God in Zion; to you our vows will be fulfilled. Psalm 65:1 (NIV)*

"Cool Down":

_____

_____

_____

_____

_____

_____

_____

God bless you muchly~

~ DAY 14 ~

Date: _____

Hello! I'm so very glad you found your way here. Amidst all life's distractions it can be easy to get off course. We are two weeks in and I commend your tenacity to keep on, keeping on dear one. Thank you. God says, …*Those who honor me I will honor*… 1 Samuel 2:30 (NIV)

Warm Up and Worship:

_____

_____

Pray Scripture: *Keep your servant also from willful sins; may they not rule over me. Then I will be blameless, innocent of great transgression. Psalm 19:13 (NIV)* Please continue in prayer that the One who is our Source of strength and peace be honored through our study today.

P.R. & P.R.

_____

_____

_____

_____

_____

_____

_____

Daily Devotional Reading: "The 'New Moon' Phase"

Recently I visited the dentist. To my shame, I was found with cavity. To my credit, I somehow made it through 3 decades of life cavity free AND the dentist did say I'm an excellent brusher. However, the dentist also said, I have really great grooves in my back molars to which the "sugar bugs" find exceptional places to hide! I must say, all was lost on me after the dentist said I had great grooves! All I could think was, "Hallelujah! This mom of six has good curves SOMEWHERE!!" You may not be able to actually SEE them since those curves reside in my back molars, but hey, we are all called to walk by faith and not sight anyway right?!! Of course this got me thinking on Scripture...

In Ezra 3:3-6 God's people have just returned to their homeland from the cavity of captivity after 70 years! Despite their fear of the foreign people around them, they begin to build again to honor God. Every morning and every evening they faithfully brought the required sacrifices. It seems they began in wholehearted devotion to prioritize their God above all. Above all fear, and uncertainty and self doubt and their questions...

What are you building, or allowing God to build through you, despite your fear of what people will think, or in spite of your fear of all you lack in your own abilities? What if, in wholehearted devotion to God you committed to step forward in faith rather than go in reverse toward regret of never having tried at all? What if you trusted God to be your Ability in your offer of availAbility to Him for such a time as this?

Reading again from Ezra 3:3-6 we can gather God's people celebrated!! Yes, in their fear and uncertainty they celebrated! Our God is our warrior through worship and they celebrated His faithfulness to provide in their wilderness seasons of the past (also known as the Feast of Tabernacles) which emboldened their faith to trust Him in their present!

How are you offering a sacrifice of praise in your current season of life? What can you recall of His faithfulness to you in your past that will help you find your faith in your present?

This Ezra passage also mentions the new moon celebrations. This was a time that God's people dedicated the new month to their God! The thing is that other pagan nations worshiped the moon. God's people held their celebrations during what is called the "New Moon" phase. Did you know that at the "New Moon" phase of the lunar cycle the moon can not be seen at all?!! God's people can worship the Creator even when the creatED cannot be seen.

Dear one our faithful God is moving for our good and His glory even when the numbers don't add up, even if the results are negative, even though things seem to have gone left rather than right - our God is still on a right for you! If you feel you are in a "New Moon" phase and having to trust beyond what your finite senses can make sense of. So were the people in Ezra 3 and yet in faith they moved forward though the foundations of the LORD's temple had NOT YET been laid. There is living hope in "not YET". ... *"What no eye has seen, what no ear has heard, and what no human mind has conceived"* - *the things God has prepared for those who love him*- 1 Corinthians 2:9 (NIV)

Don't give up because you can't see the "moon", lift your eyes, for the SON is always there.

~ ~ ~

Study in the Psalms: Today we will be reading Psalms 66, 67, 68, 69 and 70.

- Converse with God as you read through each Psalm.
- Pause and reflect on verses that catch your heart's attention.
- Record one verse from each Psalm that holds impact for you.
- Review your list. Is there a theme in the verses you highlighted? Take time and listen for God's voice to your heart.

- My favorite verse from Psalm 66:

_____

_____

_____

- My favorite verse from Psalm 67:

_____

_____

_____

- My favorite verse from Psalm 68:

  _____

  _____

  _____

- My favorite verse from Psalm 69:

  _____

  _____

  _____

- My favorite verse from Psalm 70:

  _____

  _____

  _____

Five points to ponder after reading Psalms 66-70 today.

- "Come and see!", beckons verse 5 of Psalm 66. How are our lives speaking a "come and see" invitation for the sphere of our God given influence to know Him? Verse 6 is remembering God's deliverance of the Israelites through the parting of the Red Sea (Exodus 14). Exodus 14:10-12 holds a VERY different tune from these shouts of praise over God's faithfulness in their trial! Just as Psalm 66:10 reminds us that it's often in the trials that we grow in faith, coming to know more of God's faithful character! Our God is good, the One who works to keep our feet from slipping, guiding us, teaching us, instructing us (Psalm 32:8). He is the only One who can preserve our lives having overcome death (1 Corinthians 15:55-57). We will experience trials and tribulations

BUT as Psalm 66:12 reminds us, God always brings us through, always! *When you pass through the waters, I will be with you; and when you pass through the rivers, they will not sweep over you. When you walk through the fire, you will not be burned; the flames will not set you ablaze. Isaiah 43:2 (NIV)* Our mindset must encompass beyond this life into the next which for us finite creatures is impossible without God's help to trust beyond what our physical eyes can see. However it's then that our spiritual vision has a chance to improve! *Romans 12:2 (NIV) Do not conform to the pattern of this world, but be transformed by the renewing of your mind. Then you will be able to test and approve what God's will is -his good, pleasing and perfect will.* Dear one, His will IS good, pleasing and perfect, we must not loose faith because we can't understand, it will involve trust. (See 1 Corinthians 13:12) Psalm 66:10-12 reminds me life is a gift, not a right, and so rightly should not be taken for granted. Psalm 66:5 has that exclamation to "come and see" now in verse 16 we read "come and hear"! Are we proclaiming His faithfulness with our mouth along side matching actions that show what we know of Him?! We touched yesterday on the confession of sin to clear the conduit of prayer. Psalm 66:17-20 reminds us of the importance of living with an attitude of heart that desires to obey and regularly submit to a Psalm 139:23-24 check up, humbly submitting to anything found needing confession and repentance. *Psalm 19:12-13 (NIV) But who can discern their own errors? Forgive my hidden faults. Keep your servant also from willful sins; may they not rule over me. Then I will be blameless, innocent of great transgression.*

- Psalm 67:1 wants blessing from God…why?; see verse 2, so that the world would know Him. We are blessed to be a blessing! Almost every verse in this Psalm speaks of the whole world, the nations… Verse 6, and the land yields a harvest. Doesn't this sound like the Great Commission (see Matthew 28:19-20)? Those of us who know Jesus are blessed to know Him!! We are to go out into the world, the harvest field, and share the blessing of Him that we know! We don't have to worry about sharing what we don't know, just share what you do! What a tragedy to do nothing at all because you feel you can only do a little. A little placed in God's hands can go a LOOONG way (See John 6)! *Matthew 9:37-38 (NIV) Then he said to his disciples, "The harvests plentiful but the workers are few. Ask the Lord of the harvest, therefore, to send out workers into his harvest field."* The harvest is plentiful… there are more ready to receive the blessing you have of Him than you might think. I love John 12:32 (NIV) which reminds me success lays in His hands. We don't have to be experts, we are just to lift the name of Jesus high with our lives and He Himself will do the drawing of peoples hearts to Himself! *And I, when I am lifted up from the earth, will draw all people to myself."* So don't be afraid (see Deuteronomy 31:6) you are not of those that shrink back but those who step forward in faith (see Hebrews 10:39).

- Psalm 68:19 reminds us God daily bears our burdens. If it's on our mind it's on God's heart too. *Matthew 11:28 (NIV) "Come to me, all you who are weary and burdened, and I will give you rest.* I wonder if at times the things we are tempted to call our weakness is really only weary. In Christ we are mighty, we are strong, we are overcomers but not weak, because He turns our weakness into strengths (2 Corinthians 12:9)! When the enemy try's to take you down with lies of weakness stand on Truth, be reminded of *1 John 4:4 (NIV) You, dear children, are from God and have overcome them, because the one who is in you is greater than the one who is in the world.* You will never face anything that is greater than the One with whom you face it with! Another Truth to steady your footing in what feels like weakness is *Romans 8:11 (NIV) And if the Spirit of him who raised Jesus from the dead is living in you, he who raised Christ from the dead will also give life to your mortal bodies because of his Sprit who lives in you.* When you feel threatened with weakness maybe you are just weary and you need to heed the beckoning call of Jesus in *Mark 6:31 (NIV) … "Come with me by your selves to a quiet place and get some rest."* Psalm 68:9 finds God refreshing the weary. When you are weary how much are you really doing effectively? Not much. And yet our good Heavenly Father knows, sees, cares and reaches out to provide refreshment when we are weary. Psalm 68:35 also reminds me of Psalm 29:11. Our God is our Source of strength, power and peace. Too often we run to resources and freak out when those run dry, forgetting all too easily that our God is not a resource but rather The Source of all resources and He never runs dry!

- Psalm 69 reveals a very devastated David, and yet he continued to pray. May we learn no matter how many turn against us never to turn from the One who will never turn from us. *Keep your lives free from the love of money and be content with what you have, because God has* said, *"Never will I leave you; never will I forsake you." Hebrews 13:5 (NIV)* This Psalm is one of the most quoted throughout the New Testament. For example, verse 4 is reflected in John 15:25 in reference to Jesus' suffering as is verse 21 seen in John 19:28-29. Verse 9 also reflects a scene involving Jesus in John 2:14-17. Verses 12-13 are restated by Paul in Romans 11:9-10 in regards to unbelieving Jews. Peter quotes verse 25 in Acts 1:20 which also includes Psalm 109:8. The book of life referenced in verse 28 can also be seen referred to in Revelation 3:5, 20:15 and 21:22-27. *"Every word of God is flawless; he is a shield to those who take refuge in him. Proverbs 30:5 (NIV)* The Bible is its own best commentary on itself! It aligns flawlessly and can be trusted completely. Don't let your seasons of drought make you doubt it (see Jeremiah 17:7-8).

- Psalm 70 holds a short seemingly desperate almost panicked prayer and yet David does not forget praise! How often do we remember to praise God in our panic?! I wonder if we did, we might have more peace producing patience?! This Psalm definitely seems to want God to hurry up and yet we must remember faith in God also means faith in His timing. *But do not forget this one thing, dear friends: With the Lord a day is like a thousand years, and a thousand years are like a day. 2 Peter 3:8 (NIV)* John 11 has Jesus on another seemingly delay and yet He was right on time to produce a mighty miracle. There is always purpose when Jesus says, "wait." *Yet the LORD longs to be gracious to you; therefore he will rise up to show you compassion. For the LORD is a God of justice. Blessed are all who wait for him! Isaiah 30:18 (NIV)*

"Cool Down": Record the greatest impression God made on your heart today that will encourage your relationship with Him to flourish.

_____

_____

_____

_____

_____

_____

_____

God bless you muchly~

~ DAY 15 ~

Date: _____

Hello and welcome! I'm ready for our warm up to begin! I just walked my children to the bus stop in 3 degree weather!! However the sun is shining and sparkling off all the ice crystals that have formed on every tree branch! *Awake, my soul! Awake, harp and lyre! I will awaken the dawn. I will praise you, Lord, among the nations; I will sing of you among the peoples. For great is your love reaching to the heavens; your faithfulness reaches to the skies. Be exalted, O God, above the heavens; let your glory be over all the earth. Psalm 57:8-11 (NIV)* Nothing like a balmy 3 degrees to remind you you're alive!! Awake, my soul! I praise Him for awakening our souls once more today!!

Warm Up and Worship: Record your praise for today.

_____

_____

Pray Scripture: *Rejoice in the Lord always. I will say it again: Rejoice! Philippians 4:4 (NIV)* Thank you Lord for multiple reminders and opportunities to take up a spirit of rejoicing in our salvation and our blessings. ... Please continue to open in prayer that God reveal Himself and by His grace help us understand what we read in His Word and that He grant us the ability and desire to live it out.

P.R. & P.R.

_____

_____

_____

_____

_____

_____

_____

_____

_____

_____

Daily Devotional Reading: "A Flood Of Refreshment"

The law of the Lord is perfect, refreshing the soul. The statutes of the Lord are trustworthy, making wise the simple. Psalm 19:7 (NIV)

Exodus 2:23-25 (NIV) matches 4 expressions of suffering by the people, with God's compassionate responses. The people are recorded having... "Groaned", "cried out", "cry for help", "groaning" to which the Scriptures record... "God heard", "he remembered", "God looked", and "was concerned". Psalm 34:18 (NIV) declares, _The Lord is close to the brokenhearted and saves those who are crushed in spirit._ Dear one, God shows no favoritism (Romans 2:11) and longs to meet you where you are at and be to you the all sufficient provision of everything you need. Yet in the flood of your need that threatens your drowning at times where do you flee for the filling and refreshing of your soul?

Exodus 2:15 (NIV) finds a man having fled to the side of a well after fleeing from a flood of fear. *…but Moses fled from Pharaoh and went to live in Midian, where he sat down by a well.* Dear one, if you need to flee, flee to the water of God's Word, that His Truth would flood your heart, reviving your soul. If we root down in the rule and reign of Jesus Christ and embrace His Sovereignty as our grounding point in all situations and circumstances, streams of Living Water will flow from within us! *Whoever believes in me, as Scripture has said, rivers of living water will flow from within them." John 7:38 (NIV)*

A few verses forward from Moses' seat beside the well finds us in Exodus 2:17 in which Moses is now administering water to others! *A generous person will prosper; whoever refreshes others will be refreshed. Proverbs 11:25 (NIV)* One thing leads to another and the refreshing word flows to the point that the one who once was fleeing from fractured dynamics is now found flourishing within family! *God sets the lonely in families, he leads out the prisoners with singing; but the rebellious live in a sun scorched land. Psalm 68:6 (NIV) Come near to God and he will come near to you. Wash your hands, you sinners, and purify your hearts, you double-minded. James 4:8 (NIV) Repent, then, and turn to God, so that your sins may be wiped out, that times of refreshing may come from the Lord, Acts 3:19 (NIV)*

Today, may we run to the only One who can revive, renew, restore and redeem our lives, our hope, our situation, by the well of Truth that flows to us via the living water of His refreshing Word.

So do not fear, for I am with you; do not be dismayed, for I am your God. I will strengthen you and help you; I will uphold you with my righteous right hand.
Isaiah 41:10 (NIV)

Study in the Psalms: Today we will be reading Psalms 71, 72, 73, 74 and 75.

- Converse with God as you read through each Psalm.
- Pause and reflect on verses that catch your heart's attention.
- Record one verse from each Psalm that holds impact for you.
- Review your list. Is there a theme in the verses you highlighted? Take time and listen for God's voice to your heart.

- My favorite verse from Psalm 71:

_____

_____

_____

- My favorite verse from Psalm 72:

_____

_____

_____

- My favorite verse from Psalm 73:

_____

_____

_____

- My favorite verse from Psalm 74:

_____

_____

_____

- My favorite verse from Psalm 75:

_____

_____

_____

Five points to ponder.

- I would have a hard time picking just one verse from Psalm 71 to write down, I really like verses 14-19! Maybe if I would write very, very small I could get them all in on three lines?! Let's highlight verse 8 for a moment. What is the mouth full of? In the NIV it is stated, _My mouth is full of your praise, declaring your splendor all day long._ Compare that to verse 8 in chapter 3 of James and we might have a cure for that restless tongue! Keeping our mouths full and our tongues busy with praising the splendor of our King and we might not be speaking or spewing the deadly poison that otherwise is possible from us all!

- Psalm 72 closes book two of the groupings of Psalms. We see a prayer for the king to lead well. It is always good to keep our leaders in all arenas of life in prayer. _2 Chronicles 7:14 (NIV) if my people, who are called by my name, will humble themselves and pray and seek my face and turn from their wicked ways, then I will hear from heaven, and I will forgive their sin and will heal their land._ Most likely this Psalm was written by David for his son Solomon however it looks forward to the eternal reign of our God. Psalm 72:17 speaks of our God's reign forever which will come to fulfillment at His return.

Revelation 11:15 (NIV) ... "The kingdom of the world has become the kingdom of our Lord and of his Messiah, and he will reign for ever and ever."

- Psalm 73 begins what is considered the third grouping or book of Psalms which will include Psalms 73-89. Psalm 73 is one of my favorites because of verse 17. This Psalm addresses what so many wonder about. Why does it seem the wicked prosper or the "good" suffer? In reality none of us are "good" and we all deserve hell for eternity BUT by the goodness and grace of our God we have been redeemed, set free from death, sin and the devil!! It was in verse 17 of Psalm 73 that this psalmist realized Truth and where was he exactly?! In the sanctuary of God!! When we come into His presence, when we commune with Jesus at the foot of His cross and remember His sacrifice and His victory our perspective is perfected with an eternal backdrop! I appreciate Psalm 73:15 as well because the psalmist was careful about where he declared his doubts and gratefully so, because after finding clarity he realized he could have caused others to stumble in confusion. It is important to wrestle out with God our true and honest feelings but also to be mindful of who and at what point we express those feelings to others for a number of reasons. Psalm 73:21-26 is so humbling to me. The psalmist admits his beastliness before God and YET he says, and YET God you still kept me! By His amazing grace He keeps us all even when we act like senseless, brute beasts before Him! The psalmist concludes in verses 27 and 28 with what reminds me of how Jesus phrased the benefit of unfazed commitment in *Matthew 11:6 (ESV) And blessed is he who is not offended by me."* Jeremiah 29:11 declares that God knows the plans and they are good. We will be blessed if we just trust… even when we don't understand.

- Psalm 74 follows the destructive event of the Babylonian invasion of Jerusalem. The people are in great distress and yet the concern of the prayer is over God's great name (verse 10)! May the focus of my concerns be the reverence and lifting high of His great name. Keep on to Psalm 75 and Hope is revealed once more!

- Psalm 75:2 reveals He is in control and He is on His perfect plan that cannot be thwarted (Job 42:2)! Faith in God includes faith in His timing that is always, always perfection. *Psalm 75:1 (NLT) God says, "At the time I have planned, I will bring justice against the wicked.* Doubting God's timing, His wisdom and taking matters into our own hands always leads to disaster in the end. As my children learn to drive I've told them (as we wait at difficult road crossings for traffic to clear) that it is better to wait it out as long as needed to get a good clearing of traffic rather than to take a daring dart out hoping to make it across without an accident! It's better to sit and wait awhile rather than to end up sitting in a wheel chair for the rest of your life due to an impatience accident! *Isaiah 40:31 (ESV) but they who wait for the LORD shall renew their strength; they shall mount up with wings like eagles; they shall run and to be weary; they shall walk and not faint.* Between Psalm 75:7 and verse 9 is a breath of fresh air for the believers who can realize we are not the third person of the

Trinity!! God is able and is handling all things. Letting God be God frees us up to just sing His praises!

"Cool Down":

_____

_____

_____

_____

_____

_____

_____

Thank you muchly!

~ DAY 16 ~

Date: _____

Hello dear one, beloved of God. The word "commit" as used in the below "Pray Scripture" verse (Psalm 37:5) is actually the Hebrew word galal. It literally means to roll, or even trust. God want's us to continue to roll with Him, to roll our way, thoughts, ambitions, worries, fears… all of it, over to Him. God rolled our biggest stone away (that one in front of the tomb) so that we might experience Living Hope as we roll in relationship with Him! That tomb still stands empty dear one, so there is nothing too big to roll His way that He won't be able to overcome. So… commit or roll / trust, "it" over to the only One with the complete strength and ability to shoulder it. He loves you, trust Him to lead you well.

Warm Up and Worship:

_____

_____

Pray Scripture: *Commit your way to the LORD; trust in him and he will do this: Psalm 37:5 (NIV)* Please continue in prayer to prepare your heart and mind before God. Remember to walk with someone you must agree on two things. One, the pace you will go, and two, which direction you will walk. We set our pace to God's through prayer and we set our life's direction with His, through the reading of, and submitting to, His Word.

P.R. & P.R.

_____

_____

_____

_____

_____

_____

_____

_____

_____

_____

Daily Devotional Reading: "Choice Point"

I will instruct you and teach you in the way you should go; I will counsel you with my loving eye on you. Psalm 32:8 (NIV)

We will encounter choice-points throughout our days that will afford us opportunities to follow God's leadership onto fresh trails of adventure! Exciting, right!! Unfortunately, many opportunities will be missed in the cesspools of hesitation and doubt. Acts 10 affords us encouragement in discernment.

God is about to do a new thing in Acts 10 and Peter (unbeknownst to himself) positions himself to be a part of the adventure as he continues in faithfulness in the mundane routine of his day. Sometimes faithfulness in the mundane is the hardest thing! Yet verses 9-10 indicate Peter went to the rooftop to just pray... but he got distracted by his hunger. Ever find your best laid efforts being distracted or interrupted?! Take heart dear one, God cannot be distracted from His purpose in your life! We find that God even worked through Peter's distraction within Peter's faithfulness to pursue God's heart! It is never about being good enough or trying hard enough. We cannot earn God's favor. Praise God it is by grace through faith we are saved and even our faith is God's gift to us!! (Ephesians 2:8)

God speaks a powerful message through Peter's hunger (his distraction) to which Peter responds, *"No, Lord,"*... (Acts 10:14 NLT). This statement contradicts itself, for how can we say, "No" to someone we address as "Lord"?! If God is truly Lord of our lives our answer to His call will only ever be in holy reverent submission. Yet we see God's patient endurance and lavish grace with our shortcomings all through Scripture. Praise Him! (Lamentations 3:22-23)

Verses 17-21 finds Peter very perplexed and in total confusion over the details of God's message to him YET when God says to Peter in verse 20 (NLT) , *Get up,... go...without hesitation. Don't worry, ..."* Peter engages without delay (verse 21) in the fresh trail of adventure God has for his day! Peter has spent time in the mundane moments of life getting to know and trust his life's Guide. Peter knows God to be able to lead clearly even in his cloud of confusion, one step at a time! (Proverbs 3:5-6, Isaiah 43:19)

Peter is led to an encounter with an individual (Cornelius) who is a "good" man by anyone's standards. Yet Acts 10 underlines once more that no amount of our "good" efforts win right standing with God. Peter's fresh trail of adventure leads him to sharing the good news of Jesus Christ with Cornelius. Now Cornelius is faced with a choice-point of his own and he too chooses to receive fresh new life adventure as he places his trust in Jesus as his Savior! (2 Corinthians 5:17, Romans 8:1) The ultimate choice-point in every person's life! (John 3:16, John 14:6)

You, dear one, were built for adventure... but not to go it alone. At every choice-point today we can choose to let God Almighty take point on our trail; then our biggest and best adventure is yet to come! *The LORD himself goes before you and will be with you; he will never leave you nor forsake you. Do not be afraid; do not be discouraged."* *Deuteronomy 31:8 (NIV)*

Study in the Psalms: Today we will be reading Psalms 76, 77, 78, 79 and 80.

- Converse with God as you read through each Psalm.
- Pause and reflect on verses that catch your heart's attention.
- Record one verse from each Psalm that holds impact for you.
- Review your list. Is there a theme in the verses you highlighted? Take time and listen for God's voice to your heart.

- My favorite verse from Psalm 76:

_____

_____

_____

- My favorite verse from Psalm 77:

_____

_____

_____

- My favorite verse from Psalm 78:

_____

_____

_____

- My favorite verse from Psalm 79:

_____

_____

_____

- My favorite verse from Psalm 80:

_____

_____

_____

Five points to ponder.

- Psalm 76 seems to celebrate a victory! Verse 10 speaks of human defiance bringing God praise. At first that may seem odd and yet remembering back to the plagues on Egypt as they continued to defy God (Exodus 7-11) this only reveals God's ultimate power and leads to His absolutely astounding victory over the entire situation that will be remembered through all of time!!

- Psalm 77 holds one of my favorite verses! Verse 19 and I'll quote it from the NLT. *Your road led through the sea, your pathway through the mighty waters- a pathway no one knew was there!* When we see no way our God is able dear one, to find a path that no one knew about!! A few other verses to remind us that He is able are as follows: Jude 1:24; Daniel 3:17; Matthew 3:9; Romans 4:20-21; 2 Corinthians 9:7-8; Ephesians 3:20-21; 2 Timothy 1:12; Hebrews 2:18; Hebrews 7:25 - And when He is able, but chooses not to, we must trust that He will make us able to walk the pathway He provides in His faithful presence. His way will always be our perfect way even if we can't comprehend it from our finite perspective. Just as Psalm 77:6-10 is righted by verse 11 when the psalmist recalls just Who God is and that all His ways are good and holy, always wholly for our good too, dear one.

- Psalm 78 is a sort of hymn for our homes, advising the instruction of our children, the next generation in the ways of faith in Jesus. Psalm 78:5-7 tells us to teach our children so that they will have the Hope that rises above all our worldly trials (John 16:33). What a privilege, what a purpose of grand proportions! Read the Word to know the Word so that you can live it, share it, speak it, changing the world! *Romans 10:17 (NIV) Consequently, faith comes from hearing the message, and the message is heard through the word about Christ.* Psalm 78:14 reminds that even when we can't see, in the dead of night, He is still leading faithfully. *Psalm 78:19 (NLT) They even spoke against God himself, saying, "God can't give us food in the wilderness.* And yet glancing at Genesis 43:16 we see that indeed God can and did bring about a feast in the desert and not only that but He did it during a famine!!! How often do we forget God and grieve His heart in numerous ways, seeking Him for what we can get rather than for Who He is (Psalm 78:36)?! And yet He still shows grace and mercy not treating us as our sins deserve (Psalm 78:38-39 and Psalm 103:10-14)!! Psalm 78:70-72 shows a man after God's own heart willing to be active right were God had him placed. Though David would be a king he learned to shepherd well in the training ground of the sheep pen. Where does God have you right now? Maybe it's your training ground… train hard, train well and lead in the sphere of influence He's given you. Keep the fire of His Word stoked in your heart. You have a baton to pass dear one, the next generation must catch the flame of faith! *Psalm 78:72 (NLT) He cared for them with a true heart and led them with skillful hands.* As my Shepherd cares for me like this I receive the equipping to care for others in the same way. Thus reflecting His heart to a lost and hurting generation. *How, then, can they call on the one they have not believed in? And how can they believe in the one of whom they have not heard? And how can they hear without someone preaching to them? And how can anyone preach unless they are sent? As it is written: "How beautiful are the feet of those who bring good news!" Romans 10:14-15 (NIV)*

- Psalm 79 is a Psalm for when all is going wrong, and it was, for these people due to their own sin and rebellion. When we experience devastation due to sin may it produce in us a godly sorrow. *2 Corinthians 7:10 (NIV) Godly sorrow brings repentance that leads to salvation and leaves no regret, but worldly sorrow brings death.*

Romans 6:23 (NIV) For the wages of sin is death, but the gift of God is eternal life in Christ Jesus our Lord. 1 John 1:9 (NIV) If we confess our sins, he is faithful and just and will forgive us our sins and purify us from all unrighteousness. Acts 3:19 (NIV) Repent, then, and turn to God, so that your sins may be wiped out, that times of refreshing may come from the Lord,

- Psalm 80:7-8 reminds me of John 15 and the pruning God does in our lives. *John 15:1-2 (NIV) "I am the true vine, and my Father is the gardener. He cuts off every branch in me that bears no fruit, while every branch that does bear fruit he prunes so that it will be even more fruitful.* The analogy of cutting off branches in my life sounds painful! But if there are parts that are causing unfruitfulness to occur I want to submit to the Gardner I know that wants to see me thrive! What about the "branches" in my life that are producing?! What?! A pruning?! That doesn't sound painless either!! When a good coach sees an athlete with potential they don't just leave them be. No! You drill and drive to refine those skills into their highest potential! Same is true with our lives. God sees who He made us to be, He knows the plans, the things planned long ago for us to do that would bring Him glory (Ephesians 2:10). He knows the things that gotta go and the things that need to grow. Let's not settle for easy, or comfortable when extraordinary is on God's agenda dear one.

"Cool Down":

_____

_____

_____

_____

_____

_____

_____

Thank you for your diligence and persistence in the study of our God's heart through your time in His Word. May you experience a flourishing strength fostered in your spirit through His!

~ DAY 17 ~

Date: _____

Hello dear one, this morning I was up to my elbows in hot glue and numerous other crafting materials! This craft called for a repeated action of over 100 times! How often have we found ourselves stuck in sin like hot glue?! (I mean that stuff STICKS and STINGS it's a wonder I have any fingerprints left at all!!) And yet 1, 2, 3 even 100 plus times God will forgive, redeem, restore as only His fingerprint on our heart can; if only we will turn to Him in prayer. If you are tangled in the strings of sin like "hot glue", there is One to whom you can turn to help throw off all the sin that so easily entangles (Hebrews 12:1). *John 8:36 (NIV) So if the Son sets you free, you will be free indeed.* Oh praise God for the freedom found freely in Christ!

Warm Up and Worship:

_____

_____

Pray Scripture: *Oh LORD of Heaven's Armies, what joy for those who trust in you. Psalm 84:12 (NLT)* Thank you Heavenly Father for taking care of all humanities greatest need, the forgiveness of all sin! … Please continue in prayer as we embark on this moment of fresh beginnings in Jesus.

P.R. & P.R.

_____

_____

_____

_____

_____

_____

_____

_____

_____

_____

Daily Devotional Reading:
"God's extraordinary love is for YOU!"

Our ability to share the extraordinary love of Christ with others hinges on how much we have actually accepted it for ourselves. *Dear friends, since God so loved us, we also ought to love one another. 1 John 4:11 (NIV)* We can't give what we don't have, no matter how much we would like to! Genuine gifting of the extraordinary authentic love of Christ is given through receiving, dear one.

Mark 5:1-20 reminds me of His extraordinary love for… the one. In this passage Jesus purposefully crosses a raging storm to reach a land most Jews probably never listed on their desired places of destination. In this passage Jesus encounters a man, an outcast and yet this man, this outcast was Jesus' very reason for coming! This man was living among the tombs, naked, possessed by evil and bloodied from all the cutting he was inflicting upon himself. This man was wild and violent, no human could get through to him anymore and yet Jesus came through a storm without, to calm the storm within this man. One encounter with Christ Himself and this man is completely restored, made new, he walks free of the tombs!! *Therefore, if anyone is in Christ, the new creation has come: The old has gone, the new is here! 2 Corinthians 5:17 (NIV)*

Jesus purposefully crossed all boundaries of time and space as we know it to enter into the raging brokenness of our world to seek and save the lost (Luke 19:10). This passage proves that He would have gone to the effort even if it had only been me; if it had only been you. Do you believe that Truth?!! I pray you do, dear one.

Jesus became the outcast, tortured, stripped, bloodied even crucified and placed in a tomb. He took the place of this man in the passage, He took the place of me; of you. So that by His wounds we could be healed! Jesus' tomb stands empty to this day so that by His life we can live in Hope that will never die (1 Peter 1:3)!! *But he was pierced for our transgressions, he was crushed for our iniquities; the punishment that brought us peace was on him, and by his wounds we are healed. Isaiah 53:5 (NIV)*

This man in our Mark 5 passage becomes so rejuvenated by the life and love of Christ that he changes his city through the outflow of Christ's love in him! Dear one, Jesus came for YOU that YOU might experience His unconditional and lavish love for YOU, His beloved. This encounter between the demon possessed man and Jesus is recorded three different times in the Bible! He doesn't want you to miss the point that He came to save YOU! This side of the cross the victory is won! God fought for YOU and now His victory is YOURS for the accepting! *Greater love has no one than this: to lay down one's life for one's friends. John 15:13 (NIV)*

Jesus is the Savior of the whole world and yet is still a God willing to enter the storm to still His child with His overcoming love.

"Because I love YOU." -Jesus (Isaiah 43:4)

~~~

Study in the Psalms: Today we will be reading Psalms 81, 82, 83, 84 and 85.

- Converse with God as you read through each Psalm.
- Pause and reflect on verses that catch your heart's attention.
- Record one verse from each Psalm that holds impact for you.
- Review your list. Is there a theme in the verses you highlighted? Take time and listen for God's voice to your heart.

- My favorite verse from Psalm 81:

_____

_____

_____

- My favorite verse from Psalm 82:

_____

_____

_____

- My favorite verse from Psalm 83:

  _____

  _____

  _____

- My favorite verse from Psalm 84:

  _____

  _____

  _____

- My favorite verse from Psalm 85:

  _____

  _____

  _____

Five points shared.

- As I write this it is the month of January, the beginning of a new year. Psalm 81 was recited at the feast of Trumpets or the beginning of the Jewish new year. At the start of our new year we too typically reflect over the past and look toward the future with renewed hope. Psalm 81:5 (NIV) finishes with, _I heard an unknown voice say:_ As we walk through our years day by day we will continuously hear voices pulling us this way and that, vying for presiding influence in our lives. I don't want the voice of the Author of my life to go unrecognized by me! In fact I pray His voice of Truth would be the loudest thing in my mind and heart and that it is what I long to obey every step of the way! Time in

His Word is one sure way to get to know His voice. *John 10:27 (NIV) My sheep listen to my voice; I know them, and they follow me.* A good relationship requires good communication. Our Shepherd is speaking; are we listening… following? Psalm 81:10 reminds us God longs to bless us. However if we are allowing other things to have our hearts affection and minds attention we just might miss the opportunities and open doors He is bringing us to. At this feast of Trumpets the real reason for celebrating is bought out in this Psalm. Do we keep the focus of our celebrations (Easter, Christmas…) where it needs to be? Have we allowed this worlds commercialism to creep in and steal the precious gift of refocused refreshment God designed those times to be?! Every day you wake up is the beginning of a new year if you want to look at it that way. So this year let's be intentional about knowing His voice and choosing to follow His direction, for in Him we will find our life's grandest celebration; one we don't want to miss!

- Psalm 82 deals with the judgment of judges. 1 Timothy 2:1-2 urges us to pray for our leaders, for those in authority so that it may go well for us. All people benefit from the integrity of good moral leaders. Psalm 82:6 refers to these judges as gods due to their authority over others. However God (capital G) is the Author of all authority and there is no greater leader who can stand taller, stronger, then the own who first bows before Him. Jesus in John 10:34-36 quotes this passage in Psalms. He was arguing His point that if people were called god's that ruled with authority on earth how could it be blasphemous if the True Son of God claimed deity!

- Psalm 83 is a cry for victory, a rescue, at the hand of God against enemies too powerful for their nation, God's people. The psalmist prays in verse 16 that the enemy be disgraced or covered in shame so that they would seek Him, submitting to the one true God. I pray that in our own stubborn ignorance we would not need to be taken so low before we turn our hearts up to Him.

- Psalm 84:11 reminds us that He doesn't give us everything we want just as a good parent doesn't give their two year old everything they ask for. Some things that two year old is asking for is truly not good for them. At two years old even if we explained the why behind the "no" they often would not understand. Often even if God explained the "no" to our desires it would probably only drum up more questions within our finite understanding of the infinite knowledge of God. It's best just to trust the omniscient One, He who is all-knowing! Verse 11 indicates God does give us all good things so we can know and trust that Truth. He gives us what we need to walk in obedience to Him but we must do the walking. God will give us all we need to bring Him the most glory with our lives. We will lack nothing to do that. This psalmist is longing for the fulfillment of his soul of which he has found can only be satisfied in the presence of God. May we too remember our soul is satisfied, most refreshed, in the presence of God, through His Living Word. It's not in that TV show, or that desert, or that relationship or activity... Psalm 84:3 touches my heart.

Even the sparrow considered small and worthless finds a home in the Father's heart. The swallow who's weak feet make it restless finds rest in the nest of the Father's best! If you feel weak, worthless know you are pricelessly valued in the strength of the Father's love for you. You belong, you are wanted, rest and refresh in Him dear one.

- There is nothing humans need more than the forgiveness of our sin. Psalm 85 acknowledges that God has forgiven all sin (verse 2)! *1 John 2:2 (NIV) He is the atoning sacrifice for our sins, and not only for ours but also for the sins of the whole world.* Hebrews 4:16 then reminds us we can approach His throne of grace with confidence and receive mercy and grace in our time of need!! When are we humans without need?!! So we must always be seeking His presence for He is our Vine, the fulfiller of all our needs! Apart from Him we can do nothing (John 15:5)!

"Cool Down":

_____

_____

_____

_____

_____

_____

_____

Thank you for your diligence and persistence to grow in God's Word. *Faithfulness springs forth from the earth, and righteousness looks down from heaven. Psalm 85:11(NIV)*

I hope you are feeling a flourishing within your heart dear one. God bless you muchly~

~ DAY 18 ~

Date: _____

Welcome and thank you for continuing to keep on with me in God's Word! ... *"The Lord is with you, mighty warrior." Judges 6:12 (NIV)*

Warm Up and Worship:

_____

_____

Pray Scripture: *Teach me your way, LORD, that I may rely on your faithfulness; give me an undivided heart, that I may fear your name. Psalm 86:11 (NIV)* Please continue in prayer as you prepare your heart and mind to meet with your Savior.

P.R. & P.R.

_____

_____

_____

_____

_____

_____

_____

_____

_____

_____

Daily Devotional Reading: "In Every Season - All The Time"

The book of Ecclesiastes in the Bible reminds us our God is the Author of all time and seasons. We learn that, *What has been will be again, what has been done will be done again; there is nothing new under the sun. Ecclesiastes 1:9* Now we can perceive this verse from down in "Eeyore's Pit" or from the top of "Tiggers Triumph".

We can rationalize that if nothing's new or going to be new under the sun and really, if you look at it, socially, politically, emotionally… we humans tend to cycle on the hamster wheel! (Case in point: Back then decrees were made to social distance from the lepers, now decrees are made to social distance for other diseases…nothing new really.)

OR we can rationalize that if nothing is new under the sun, and the Son of God still reigns the same yesterday, today and forever, then our good God remains the Author of all time and seasons, all His promises are steadfast and nothing reigns over our conquering King! **No oppression, depression, tragedy, failure, sickness or setback can set His child back in Him!! He still fights for family, still shelters the weak, still revives the weary, provides for the poor! He still breaks the chains of strongholds and pierces darkness with Light, He is still leading His own in triumphant victory because He is the Victorious One!!**

Ears to hear and eyes to see - both are gifts from the LORD. Proverbs 20:12 (NLT) Unwrap the gift of His Almighty perspective for His filter is always through Living Hope dear one!

As we speak of seasons and perspectives, today my children left for school (for the first time this season) in fall attire, for change is in the air! There is a crispness to the morning now that revives the senses as you step outside. It's as if God is grabbing our attention to remind us in all your "seasons" and at all times, He is moving, working for our good and His glory! Will we take time to notice?!

As we observe the changing of the seasons in the air from summer to fall we take note that this change only leads to the deadness of winter. Again another opportunity to sit in "Eeyore's Pit" or jump on "Tiggers Triumphant" perspective! What we may perceive as "dead" is really only a season of REST while God continues to work the miraculous!!!

The LORD directs our steps, so why try to understand everything along the way? Proverbs 20:24 (NLT) As my mom reminded me this morning, it's not joy that makes us grateful; it's gratitude that makes us joyful and when we rest in the powerful Truth of His unfailing Word in every season, we can rise triumphantly unshaken, all the time.

~~~

Study in the Psalms: Today we will be reading Psalms 86, 87, 88, 89 and 90.

- Converse with God as you read through each Psalm.
- Pause and reflect on verses that catch your heart's attention.
- Record one verse from each Psalm that holds impact for you.
- Review your list. Is there a theme in the verses you highlighted?

Take time and listen for God's voice to your heart.

• My favorite verse from Psalm 86:

_____

_____

_____

• My favorite verse from Psalm 87:

_____

_____

_____

• My favorite verse from Psalm 88:

_____

_____

_____

• My favorite verse from Psalm 89:

_____

_____

_____

• My favorite verse from Psalm 90:

_____

_____

_____

Five points to ponder.

• *Psalm 86:4 (NIV) Bring joy to your servant, Lord, for I put my trust in you.* The next few verses then go on through a list of reasons for trusting in the Lord. Our God is forgiving and good, abounding in love and the One who answers when we call. There is unshakable joy to be found when we root our hearts to the Truth that is eternal. Verses 11-13 are some of my favorites. It's good to note that the psalmist, in these verses is asking to be taught, not so that he could *think* about following but that so that he could! He declares that he will praise and he will glorify God's name. This is spoken with conviction, a single mind focused on the things of God. Not a, double minded, wishy washy, I'll see how I feel and what I think before I decide, mindset. Joy comes in resolutely setting our anchor of hope in the One who is not shaking whether we feel like it or not. Psalm 86:16 touches my heart as it finishes with …*save me, because I serve you just as my mother did.* Obviously his mother's faith made an impact, whether she knew it or not. Children are always watching, someone is always watching. I pray I can live out my faith as faithfully as my own mother. Verse 17 asks for a sign of God's goodness. It's fine to ask for God to reveal Himself to us. I pray Matthew 13:16 for myself and those I love all the time. "Dear God, please give us eyes to see and ears to perceive Your presence, Your love notes, Your workings… all around us." Even as we pray for more spiritual vision lets not miss the ways He has already revealed Himself, in the sunrise, the waking up of our souls again this morning, being able to hear the birds and taste our coffee in the morning, the friend that smiled on their walk by… evidence of His goodness, faithfulness and care! Amazing how our God has faithfully painted beautiful sunrises and sunsets every day since the beginning of time. He has done it whether He would receive a "thank you" or not, even when He knew another would wrongly be given the credit. He is faithful even when we are not (2 Timothy 2:13). Praise Him!

• Psalm 87 celebrates the city of God or Jerusalem and looks forward to our Heavenly Home. Heaven will be perfect, uninterrupted communion with our God. As verse 7 declares, *"All my fountains are in you."* Indeed, all that refreshes and rejuvenates and sustains is found in our God and in Heaven there will be an ever uninterrupted flow because sin, death and the devil will be no more! Flip ahead in your Bible to Revelation 21:10-27 to catch a glimpse of this glorious Heavenly Holy City of God! Did you catch in verse 21 that the streets are paved in gold! Gold is Heaven's asphalt! Can you even imagine!! We can't take our wealth with us, Heaven obviously has enough of it's own and yet God says the gift of our faith is far more valuable than gold so store up your treasure in Heaven through keeping the faith living in trust filled obedience of His Word (Matthew 6:19-21 and 1 Peter 1:7). Revelation 21:17 in my NLT indicates the walls are 216 feet thick!! The gates that fit those walls are made of pearl (verse 21)!! Remember how pearls are formed? They begin as an irritating grain of sand inside a clam. It is rubbed over and over until it is coated and smoothed into a beautiful priceless pearl - looking at an irritatingly brown lumpy sharp edged grain of sand… who would have thought?! What sized irritation did it have to be to become a pearl the size of a 216 foot thick wall?! Probably a cross sized one don't you think?! Jesus took the cross which became our way into the Kingdom!! *John 14:6 (NIV) Jesus answered, "I am the way and the truth and the life. No one comes to the Father except through me.* Revelation 21:27 (NLT) states that, *Nothing evil will be allowed to enter, nor anyone who practices shameful idolatry and dishonesty-but only those whose names are written in the Lamb's Book of Life.* Everyone is invited into the Kingdom, to have their names written down in the Book of Life through their belief in Jesus as the true Son of God our Savior of the world, dying for our sin and rising again on the third day! Who would refuse?! In this Holy City to come, *He will wipe every tear from their eyes. There will be no more death' or mourning or crying or pain, for the old order of things has passed away." Revelation 21:4 (NIV)* Heaven is too wonderful for us to comprehend so much so that this description tells us what it will not be because it's what we understand… we know tears and death… God says it will be none of that and what is will be is too wonderful to comprehend yet!! See also 1 Corinthians 6:9-11. *However, as it is written: "What no eye has seen, what no ear has heard, and what no human mind has conceived" - the things God has prepared for those who love him - 1 Corinthians 2:9 (NIV)*

- Psalm 88 is known as the saddest Psalm. It deals with despair, depression, discouragement and death, all of which is a reality in life. *John 16:33 (NIV) "I have told you these things, so that in me you may have peace. In this world you will have trouble. But take heart! I have overcome the world."* "Take heart" is an action handed to us. It is an action we can choose. We see that even though this psalmist is very, very low, possibly even close to death with many unanswered questions, he still prays, he still pours his heart out to God in honesty. Our feelings are not facts and we are in trouble when we start navigating life as if they are. We must choose to seek Truth in His Word regardless of how we feel. We will always have enough strength to seek Him for more. This psalmist begins in verse one crying out to God in prayer. Where there is prayer there is lingering hope. So even though this Psalm is dark we still have the penetrating Truth to take heart, found in *John 1:5 (NIV) The light shines in the darkness, and the darkness has not overcome it.* If there is anyone who can relate to the depth of our pain it is our Savior, Jesus Christ (Hebrews 4:15). *He was despised and rejected by mankind, a man of suffering, and familiar with pain. Like one from whom people hide their faces he was disposed, and we held him in low esteem. Surely he took up our pain and bore our suffering, yet we considered him punished by God, stricken by him and afflicted. But he was pierced for our transgressions, he was crushed for our iniquities; the punishment that brought us peace was on him, and by his wounds we are healed. Isaiah 53:3-5 (NIV)* Could God have allowed such a Psalm of gloom to be included to speak to the depths of our hearts that He understands, He knows we will experience things that just seem all wrong, things we cannot understand. Who was the first on earth to experience death? Abel the worshiper - WHAT!? WHY?! But from Abel's perspective to be the first to enter eternal paradise was it a bad thing?! NO! He was probably rejoicing to be free of the worlds brokenness and in the presence of the One he worshiped well. Dear one, we cannot let the enemy get a foothold in our faith because things sometimes just do not seem to add up in our finite understanding of things.

See Isaiah 55:8-9, 1 Corinthians 13:12 and Romans 8:35-39. Choose to take heart one beat at a time for He who promised is faithful (Hebrews 10:23).

- Psalm 89 was written by Ethan the Ezrahite and according to 1 Kings 4:31 he was a pretty wise guy. This Psalm was to describe the incredible reign of David however to this day we see it point forward to the eternal reign of Jesus (Psalm 89:27, Revelation 22:5). Psalm 89:34-35 is an incredible promise that God has kept. Though Israel disobeyed and suffered consequences as God has warned for disobedience He remained faithful to His promise. The Messiah did come through the descendants of David and one day the eternal throne of God will be established for eternity upon His return. God has proven faithful throughout the ages and is the same yesterday, today and forever (Hebrews 13:8). See Hebrews 6:13-18. The beautiful thing of this Psalm is the last verse. In Psalm 89:52 the psalmist chooses to praise the Lord because He can be trusted. Our God is good, faithful and with us always through all we do not understand and cannot make sense of. Embracing faith like a child rather than childish faith will free us up to enjoy so much more of life in spite of what we cannot wrap our finite minds around in God's infinite plan.

- Psalm 90 begins book four of the Psalms including Psalms numbered 90-106. It is also the oldest Psalm in the Bible. Psalm 90:4 reminds us that God is not limited by time. The author of this Psalm was Moses and he thought he was ready to take on the world for God at 40 but God had him wait until he was 80! Our prime time will always be God's time! No matter how old or young we are, our effectiveness lays in God's hand (Psalm 90:17). According to Psalm 139:16 God has written down the number of our days so no diagnosis or tragedy can trump or steal that which God has ordained. No trial trumps God's power and plan for our next moment. "Dear God, help me to steward well that which You allow to enter into my numbered days, that my life might bring You the most glory possible." God knows the number of our days as He knows the number of hairs on our heads. We are wise to ask God to help us number or days too that we might gain a heart of wisdom (Psalm 90:12) to use our days wisely and not wastefully.

"Cool Down":

_____

_____

_____

_____

_____

_____

_____

Satisfy us in the morning with your unfailing love, that we may sing for joy and be glad all our days. Psalm 90:14 (NIV) Go sing for joy dear one for He makes us fit to flourish in every season!

~ DAY 19 ~

Date: _____

Welcome my flourishing friend! I'm grateful for you. Right now I have a young son leaning over my shoulder asking for the whereabouts to his winter gloves. Gloves like socks tend to get chucked with the utmost of strength when they are removed so finding them again continues to be challenge in our home! This reminds me that no matter how hard we may have fought it, the faithfulness of our God has never lost track of us. *You hem me in behind and before, and you lay your hand upon me. Psalm 139:5 (NIV)* Now, while you record your reason for worship today, I'm going to go search for a winter glove that has sure to have grown legs and walked to Egypt!

Warm Up and Worship:

_____

_____

Pray Scripture: *Teach us to number our days, that we may gain a heart of wisdom. Psalm 90:12 (NIV)* Please continue in prayer as you prepare your heart and mind to meet with our Creator.

P.R. & P.R.

_____

_____

_____

_____

_____

_____

_____

_____

_____

_____

Daily Devotional Reading: "Keep Me"

Keep me as the apple of your eye; hide me in the shadow of your wings
Psalm 17:8 (NIV)

"Keep me" is a plea in prayer, not because God could somehow forget to keep track of us (Hebrews 6:10, Isaiah 49:15, Psalm 139, Job 23:10, John 10:28), but rather somehow we might wander from Him (Psalm 119:176, Romans 7:15).

I did not send these prophets, yet they have run with their message; I did not speak to them, yet they have prophesied. But if they had stood in my council, they would have proclaimed my words to my people and would have turned them from their evil ways and from their evil deeds. Jeremiah 23:21-22 (NIV)

…If they had stood in my council… "Dear Heavenly Father, keep me in Your council!"

"I am the vine; you are the branches. If you remain in me and I in you, you will bear much fruit; apart from me you can do nothing. John 15:5 (NIV)

In a world full of wonderful distractions it's easy to be swayed from your greatest purpose in Christ wandering after something good. The enemy masquerades as the angel of light (2 Corinthians 11:14) not darkness! It's too easy to distinguish good from evil, much harder to distinguish good from best. Satan didn't entice Eve with eggplant back in Genesis 3 (sorry if you like eggplant) but rather a juicy sweet apple! *Be alert and of a sober mind. Your enemy the devil prowls around like a roaring lion looking for someone to devour. 1 Peter 5:8 (NIV) In addition to all this, take up the shield of faith, with which you can extinguish all the flaming arrows of the evil one. Ephesians 6:16 (NIV)*

Keep in the council of His Word and you will be kept in the Way that leads to life. *Jesus answered, "I am the way and the truth and the life. No one comes to the Father except through me. John 14:6 (NIV) The thief comes only to steal and kill and destroy; I have come that they may have life, and have it to the full. John 10:10 (NIV)*

…let the one who has my word speak it faithfully… Jeremiah 23:28 (NIV)

~~~

Study in the Psalms: Today we will be reading Psalms 91, 92, 93, 94 and 95.

- Converse with God as you read through each Psalm.
- Pause and reflect on verses that catch your heart's attention.
- Record one verse from each Psalm that holds impact for you.
- Review your list. Is there a theme in the verses you highlighted? Take time and listen for God's voice to your heart.

- My favorite verse from Psalm 91:

  _____

  _____

  _____

- My favorite verse from Psalm 92:

  _____

  _____

  _____

- My favorite verse from Psalm 93:

  _____

  _____

  _____

- My favorite verse from Psalm 94:

  _____

  _____

  _____

- My favorite verse from Psalm 95:

  _____

  _____

  _____

Five points to ponder.

- At first glance Psalm 91 may drum up many questions. For example in verse 10 when it speaks of no disaster coming near you... you may be wondering what exactly that means having experienced quite possibly a lot of disaster in life! It is when we embrace the eternal perspective through prayer, studying the Scriptures in totality, we find peace that passes our understanding. There are certainly more times than we can probably count that we have been kept from disasters we knew not even the threat of. It's just as important to praise God for the miracles as much as the things that He kept from you that would have required a miracle! 2 Timothy 4:18 reminds us we do arrive safely in His Heavenly Kingdom. It doesn't promise an easy road in. We may cannon ball in but we will nail the landing not even smelling like smoke dear one! Isaiah 54:17 reminds us that no weapon formed against us will win and backing up to verse 16 tells us that is because our God is over even the weapon maker!! Psalm 91:9 reminds us it is our choice to make the Most High our dwelling place. He is calling us all (Matthew 11:28-30) but we must choose to accept the invite. John 15:5 reminds us that He is the Vine we are the branch and that apart from Him we can do nothing. Often we see the "wine" so to speak flowing from another life and think why is all the disaster coming to me?! We too often forget when we see the beauty of the "wine" flowing from another life that wine comes from a crushing first. Grapes must be crushed to produce wine. How often do we forfeit the flow of "wine" in our life because we are too busy whining about our situation!? We whine and resist the crushing that will by His faithfulness produce an outflow of "wine" as we remain in the Vine. It is in taking up and sharing God's yoke that our crushings can bring about a flow of "wine" that will strengthen others. Often what feels like weakness looks like strength to others (2 Corinthians 12:9). Our sustaining strength is found in yoking up in relationship with our Savior. Psalm 91:14-16 is a beautiful picture of a relationship. We love Him - He rescues and protects; we acknowledge His name - He answers when we call for He is with us in trouble, delivers and satisfy us... with what? Maybe not with what we think our moment requires but upon what our eternity relies. Psalm 91:16 assures us of our ultimate need being met; salvation is guaranteed to those in love with Him.

- Psalm 92:12-15 is what this study aims to solidify in our hearts and minds. Romans 3:10 reminds us no one is righteous not even one! Yet this Psalm states it is the righteous that are fit to flourish! Those who respond to the gift of faith God has extended, repenting of their sinfulness and confessing their need for a Savior, planting themselves in Truth, in the Word of God, receiving Jesus, declaring Him as the Rock of their life, that is the one who receives HIS robes of righteousness! *God made him who had no sin to be sin for us, so that in him we might become the righteousness of God. 2 Corinthians 5:21 (NIV)* Jesus in us, by the power of His Spirit, produces the flourishing we desire for our lives. *The thief comes only to steal kill and destroy; I have come that they may have life, and have it to the full. John 10:10 (NIV) They will still bear fruit in old age, they will stay fresh and green, Psalm 91:14(NIV)* How? By, *proclaiming, "The LORD is upright; he is my Rock, and there is no wickedness in him." Psalm 91:15 (NIV)*

- *Psalm 93:4 (NLT) But mightier than the violent raging of the seas, mightier than the breakers on the shore- the LORD above is mightier than these!* Mic drop. Nothing raging in your life is over the God that reigns above it all. *Then Jesus came to them and said, "All authority in heaven and on earth has been given to me. Matthew 28:18 (NIV)* And He is always working and always for our good and His glory (John 5:17, Romans 8:28). Blessed are those who's trust and confidence remains in Him (Jeremiah 17:7). We have an anchor firm and secure, we do not have to be tossed about on the raging waves of our situation and circumstances or that of our own doubts (Hebrews 6:19). Take shelter in His name, in His great and precious promises that will hold true till the end. *Through these he has given us his very great and precious promise, so that through them you may participate in the divine nature, having escaped the corruption in the world caused by evil desires. 2 Peter 1:4 (NIV) "Every word of God is flawless; he is a shield to those who take refuge in him. Proverbs 30:5 (NIV)*

- Psalm 94 reminds me that often our greatest need is not to be informed but to be reminded! God will win the day dear one! *When I said, "My foot is slipping," your unfailing love, LORD supported. When anxiety was great within me, your consolation brought me joy. Psalm 91:18-19 (NIV)* Verse 8 wonders when we will become wise. Every day will be a battle for our single minded focus on God's Truth. The world holds out its wisdom but true wisdom is not based on age or eduction, it comes directly from God (James 1:5, Proverbs 9:10). His wisdom differs from worldly wisdom. God's wisdom is pure, peace loving, considerate, submissive, full of mercy, good fruit, sincere and impartial (James 3:17). When we choose a single minded focus on our God's Truth, when we delight ourselves in Him He will delight our hearts but we must decide if we truly want Him to change our delight to mirror His. We waffle because our flesh desires worldly ways (James 1:14). Wisdom from God will root us solid and He will pour it out generously upon us but we must wholeheartedly desire Him or we will wander and wonder without aim. Psalm 94:9-11 is a wake up call, a reminder that God knows what He is doing, don't ever doubt it. *We demolish arguments and every pretension that sets itself up against the knowledge of God, and we take captive every thought to make it obedient to Christ. 2 Corinthians 10:5 (NIV)*

• Psalm 95 lends itself to our last point. We will be tossed about in restlessness of mind and heart unless we choose to submit to our Savior's best. …*Today, if only you would hear his voice, "Do not harden your hearts… Psalm 95:7-8 (NIV) For since the creation of the world God's invisible qualities - his eternal power and divine nature - have been clearly seen, being understood from what has been made, so that people are without excuse. For although they knew God, they neither glorified him as God nor gave thanks to him, but their thinking became futile and their foolish hearts were darkened. Romans 1:20-21 (NIV)* Choosing to worship even when our mood doesn't match our mission wards off a hardened heart doomed to dark foolishness. It's when we worship we fulfill our highest calling. *Revelation 4:11 (NIV) "You are worthy, our Lord and God, to receive glory and honor and power, for you created all things, and by your will they were created and have their being."* My beating heart, the breath in my lungs proves I have reason to worship Him!

"Cool Down":

_____

_____

_____

_____

_____

_____

_____

God bless you muchly~

~ DAY 20 ~

Date: _____

We also have the prophetic message as something completely reliable, and you will do well to pay attention to it, as to a light shining in a dark place, until the day dawns and the morning star rises in your hearts. 2 Peter 1:19 (NIV)

Welcome my friend, this verse recently stood out to me. In a world full of unreliable people, places and things we have God's complete Word that is 100% reliable!! This verse further advises us then to pay attention to it like a light in a dark room. Ever been in the dark and see a laser pointer light appear? You become consumed with finding it's origin! Laser pointer lights will keep a pet entertained for HOURS because they become so fixated on the light! I imagine that is the kind of focus that brings about the fruitful life God desires for His people created in His image. The last line in 2 Peter 1:19 personally served to encourage me to continue to wrestle out the passages with God until He makes His voice clear to me. The Morning Star is Jesus and I want His Word to rise in my heart above the wind and waves of this unreliable world in all my gifted moments.

Revelation 22:16 (NIV) "I, Jesus, have sent my angel to give you this testimony for the churches. I am the Root and the Offspring of David, and the bright Morning Star." Dear one we always have a reliable Light in the dark. Your word is a lamp to my feet, a light on my path. Psalm 119:105 (NIV)

Warm Up and Worship:

_____

_____

Pray Scripture: ... _"Speak, for your servant is listening." 1 Samuel 3:10 (NIV)_ Please continue in prayer as you prepare your heart and mind to meet with our Good Shepherd.

P.R. & P.R.

_____

_____

_____

_____

_____

_____

_____

_____

_____

_____

_____

Daily Devotional Reading: "Even This"

Instead, he turned and went into his palace, and did not take even this to heart.
Exodus 7:23 (NIV)

Are we in danger of having built ourselves an impenetrable palace? A palace of problematic fear; a palace of pride; a palace of past mistakes; a palace of people pleasing facades; a palace void of any real peace?! Exodus reveals the extreme effort God made to get a message of His Sovereignty through to the Pharaoh of Egypt and time and again the Pharaoh hardened his heart.

When Pharaoh is first confronted his initial question is, "Who is the LORD…?" (Ex. 5:2) After this all his questions stem from "Why?" When we don't know Who our Sovereign Lord is the "Why's?" of this broken world will build its own impenetrable palace around our hearts. The attempt to numb the pain of all the unanswerable questions only leads to death inside the palace just as Pharaoh eventually experiences (Ex. 12).

Even those who know our Sovereign Lord can be derailed by this world's brokenness and unanswerable "why's?" if they allow their focus to drift from His precious promises to their own palace of problems. Exodus 5:9 (NIV) records the enemy saying, *Make the work harder for the people so that they keep working and pay no attention to lies.* However what the enemy was calling "lies" was really the Truth! Unfortunately his plan worked and Exodus 6 records God reminding the people of His Truth; His faithfulness throughout the generations, His mighty hand to save, His attention to their heartache, His good plan for their future and His promise to save and yet… even this could not penetrate the peoples despair. Why? Exodus 6:9 (NIV) …*but they did not listen to him because of their discouragement and harsh labor.*

Dear one, do not let the unanswerable "why's?" of this world distract you from Who you know is Sovereign and good; Who holds all the answers to the "why's?" in your heart for the day we will be able to comprehend the answers AND even thank Him for the way He worked all things together for our good (Romans 8:28)! *That is why I am suffering as I am. Yet this is no cause for shame, because I know whom I have believed, and am convinced that he is able to guard what I have entrusted to him until that day. 2 Timothy 1:12 (NIV)*

"Is God's comfort too little for you? Is his gentle word not enough? What has taken away your reason? What has weakened your vision, Job 15:11-12 (NLT)

Tuck this invitation in your heart's pocket dear one…
"Come to me, all you who are weary and burdened, and I will give you rest. Matthew 11:28 (NIV)
…and even this…
For God so loved the world that he gave his one and only Son, that whoever believes in him shall not perish but have eternal life. John 3:16 (NIV)

Don't let your "palace" keep you from His peace; …*he himself is our peace…* (Eph. 2:14)

Study in the Psalms: Today we will be reading Psalms 96, 97, 98, 99 and 100.

- Converse with God as you read through each Psalm.
- Pause and reflect on verses that catch your heart's attention.
- Record one verse from each Psalm that holds impact for you.
- Review your list. Is there a theme in the verses you highlighted? Take time and listen for God's voice to your heart.

- My favorite verse from Psalm 96:

_____
_____
_____

- My favorite verse from Psalm 97:

_____
_____
_____

- My favorite verse from Psalm 98:

_____
_____
_____

- My favorite verse from Psalm 99:

_____
_____
_____

- My favorite verse from Psalm 100:

_____

_____

_____

Five points to ponder.

- Psalm 96 begins with the encouragement to sing a new song! Not only that but it gives you lyrics for that new song! If you find yourself feeling down, this is the Psalm we need to take up. We are commissioned to declare (the NLT states it as publish in verse three) God's glorious deeds! In the writing world finding a publishing company can be brutal. Will we willingly accept God's offer to be the one to publish/declare with our lives, thoughts and words, His awesomeness!! What a privilege, what an honor that of all the ways to transform the world God chooses us to be His messengers of the Good News! Another reason to sing God's praises is that it appears (according to Job 38:4-7) God enjoys working to background music!! He is our warrior through worship let's not waste a moment longer but take up a new song, a song He has already written for us with His nail scarred hand dear one. Now, how much does the world spend on beauty treatments and strength enhancing programs?! Psalm 96:6 tells me all we need in that department (and any other department for that matter) is found in His sanctuary. Verse 8 beckons us to give, not because God Almighty needs anything from us (certainly not our money) but because in the giving, our professions are given meaning and our lives become about something bigger than me, myself and I. Giving brings the gift of a new song to our lips and a new tune to our hearts. *Deuteronomy 8:18 (NIV) But remember the LORD your God, for it is he who gives you the ability to produce wealth…* Giving reminds you of your Source which extends beyond your own resources and there is great peace in that. *Isaiah 58:10 (ESV) if you pour yourself out for the hungry and satisfy the desire of the afflicted, then shall your light rise in the darkness and your gloom be as the noonday.*

- Psalm 97 begins with the fact that the Lord reigns, He is king! The wisdom of the world will fight that at every turn. The worlds wisdom says, "you are king", and godly wisdom says, "submit to The King". Why can those of us that submit to our God, Jesus as King of kings and Lord of lords be joyful?! Because in Him we are kept safe for eternity. No matter what we go through or what we face it will never be bigger than Who we face it with. One day our God is coming back and every knee will bow before Him and every tongue will confess Him as the one true God (Philippians 2:10-11). We as believers can already begin celebrating because the Kingdom is within us (Luke 17:21)! Kind of like we live in the already but not yet… we have His faithful promises from the past to bank on with sure hope for our future which brings peace within our today.

- Psalm 98 again encourages us to take up a new song, one focused on salvation and the joy that is surely to come for He has won!! Luke 19:40 tells us if we keep quiet the stones threaten to take our praise job away!! We always, always have something to praise Him for if only that this world is not how it ends for us in Jesus! Things do not always go as we planned or had hoped. Think of Simeon in Luke 2:25-35. He was promised to see the Lord's Messiah before he died and when a poor young couple walked in with a baby he could have missed it all together! He could have missed it in a bitter pool of disappointment that it wasn't some conquering parade complete with chariots and spears and mighty men!! But Simeon embraced the unexpected miracle and was mightily blessed AND was the giver of a mighty blessing through his willingness to take up God's perspective through trust. I wonder what you might have received that has been nothing like you had planned? Are you willing to pray it out, allowing God to play it out according to His best will and way?

- Psalm 99 highlights Moses, Aaron and Samuel in verse 6 as having been faithful in their dependence of God. They turned to Him and called on Him and God answered these faithful yet flawed men. What encouragement it is to see that our God forgives and uses the flawed who continue to get up and pursue faithfulness through their trust in Who He is. *Do not gloat over me, my enemy! Though I have fallen, I will rise. Though I sit in darkness, the LORD will be my light. Micah 7:8 (NIV) The LORD came and stood there, calling as at the other times, "Samuel! Samuel!" Then Samuel said, "Speak, for your servant is listening." 1 Samuel 3:10 (NIV)* May this constantly be the prayer posture of my heart also.

- Psalm 100. WOW can you believe we have studied 100 Psalms already!! May God continue to stir a craving for His Word that cannot be satisfied but by ever increasing amounts of Him who is our Word! *In the beginning was the Word, and the Word was with God, and the Word was God. John 1:1 (NIV)* Our God is worthy of all our worship. Verse 3 says we are to know that the Lord is God and that He is our Creator. How does knowing this change things for you? He is our Creator thus we are the creation and Genesis 1:27 says we are created in His image. This gives us at least one reason to love everyone including ourselves. As Creator He holds the authority over our lives. If we do not acknowledge this we begin to act as creator of our me-centered world. Consumed with pride, greed, envy, idolatry… and then when all we have built for ourselves is taken or falls apart, so do we. When we realize we were created by design, *And God is able to bless you abundantly, so that in all things at all times, having all that you need, you will abound in every good work. 2 Corinthians 9:8 (NIV)* we can't help but want to give out of all that God has given to us. Then if all is taken away and all falls apart, we don't, because we have a Creator that remains with us and is creative enough to see us through when things are way beyond us. People become like what they worship - see Psalm 115:4-8 - another reason why God, who always wants what is best for us, desires all our worship.

"Cool Down":

_____

_____

_____

_____

_____

_____

_____

God bless you muchly~

~ DAY 21 ~

Date: _____

Hi friend. I just finished doing some baking. The weather forecast is calling for a fresh foot of snow so all the school districts have already canceled school for tomorrow. Yea!! With all my babies at home I decided to bake some pumpkin chocolate chip bread for the mornings breakfast. It will be a welcome treat after shoveling!

I have this special cross shaped cake pan so I doubled up the recipe and filled the whole pan. Upon trying to remove the baked bread from the pan… it did not remove. However I was able to piece the bread back together enough that the cross shape was still visible. I then proceeded to use my sifter to sprinkle powered sugar on top. Since it's a snow day breakfast I wanted it to look like snow. As I sprinkle sifted I began to try and cover the cracks in the cross due to the demolition removal of the cake from the pan. Now I have a cake with quite possibly more sprinkled (or shall I say, dumped) powdered sugar on top than cake itself! BUT with such a thick layer of sugar there are no cracks in sight!

This got me thinking of the affects of the true cross. *Cleanse me with hyssop, and I will be clean; wash me, and I will be whiter than snow. Psalm 51:7 (NIV)* As a believer in Jesus' sacrifice, taking my place on the cross for the debt of my sin, I am covered by the sacrificial blood of the cross! I'm set free from the chains of sin! Now, when I find myself caught in sin, I can approach the throne with humble reverence and repentance and receive redemption!! I'm made new, cleaned up white as freshly fallen snow. Like the layer of sugar on my cake, Jesus' blood is so thick and so eternal that there is no sin He cannot cover dear one.

On the cross not one of Jesus' bones was broken. Blood is produced in the bones. The supply of Jesus' redeeming blood will never run dry! What a symbol for us all that none of us, none of us is too far gone for our God to save (See John 19:33-36). *Surely the arm of the LORD is not too short to save, nor his ear too dull to hear. Isaiah 59:1 (NIV)* Oh praise Him!! That is a reason to worship!

Warm Up and Worship:

_____

_____

Pray Scripture: *Therefore, if anyone is in Christ, the new creation has come: The old has gone, the new is here! 2 Corinthians 5:17 (NIV)* Please continue in prayer as you prepare your heart and mind to meet with our Redeemer.

P.R. & P.R.

_____

_____

_____

_____

_____

_____

_____

_____

_____

_____

Daily Devotional Reading: "An Incandescently Bright Future"

"The virgin will conceive and give birth to a son, and they will call him "Immanuel" (which means "God with us"). Matthew 1:23 (NIV)

Tis the season to search high and low for the perfect gift to warm the heart of another. After finding that gift, have you ever wondered just how many steps it took you? Probably not, even though we have a plethora of devices nowadays that readily calculate our steps for us. At the end of our gift quest it's not the steps it took that consumes our focus, it's the joy of the find, the reward for having not given up in the journey, no matter how many steps it took! This brings to mind a verse in Job.

For now You number my steps… Job 14:16 (NKJV) WOW! The same God who keeps track of all our tears (Psalm 56:8) and knows the number of hairs on our head (Luke 12:7) ALSO counts our every step!! An electronic device only counts your steps if it is with you, so the very fact that God tells you He numbers your steps reminds you, in each step, every day, He is WITH you (Josh. 1:9)! Yesterday, today, and forever into the future - WITH you (Heb. 13:8)!

Our future in Jesus is incandescently bright because He lives! Isaac, Jacob, Joseph, Moses (just to name a few from the Bible) spoke blessing over future generations in spite of all their current struggles and imperfections. Their sure hope was not based on faulty humanity but rather in God's faithfulness to His flawless Word.

The word *incandescent* is defined in the dictionary: "Emitting light as a result of being heated." God declares His Word to be like fire (Jer. 23:29) so within each gifted step this new year, remember and remain wrapped in the warmth of His faithful Word, His precious promises (2 Pt. 1:4) that tell you just Who it is that cares enough to number your steps! His name is Immanuel - God with you (Matt. 1:23).

He is at work in you and around you even at this very moment (Jn. 5:17)! So, what or who is it that has your focus? You will never face anything bigger than Who (Immanuel) you face "it" with. Resting in His presence you will radiate incandescently with sure hope (Rom. 5:5)! Dear one, keep on in your quest toward the gift of your Heavenly home. Joy and strength are found experiencing God with you on the journey (Neh. 8:10). He ...*says to you, Do not fear; I will help you. Isaiah 41:13 (NIV)*

Jesus is our greatest gift that we get to keep even as we give Him away; He's the gift that can warm every heart. *"Come to me, all you who are weary and burdened, and I will give you rest. … for I am gentle and humble in heart, and you will find rest for your souls. Matthew 11:28-29 (NIV) For God so loved the world (*YOU) that he gave his one and only Son, that whoever believes in him shall not perish but have eternal life. John 3:16 (NIV)* *Insert of parenthesis mine. (YOU) are loved forever and always no matter what!

God bless you muchly dear one and best wishes as you step into this gift of a new year (each day is a beginning of a new year) filled with an incandescently bright hope for your future, because of Jesus!

Study in the Psalms: Today we will be reading Psalms 101, 102, 103, 104 and 105.

- Converse with God as you read through each Psalm.
- Pause and reflect on verses that catch your heart's attention.
- Record one verse from each Psalm that holds impact for you.
- Review your list. Is there a theme in the verses you highlighted? Take time and listen for God's voice to your heart.

- My favorite verse from Psalm 101:

_____

_____

_____

- My favorite verse from Psalm 102:

_____

_____

_____

- My favorite verse from Psalm 103:

_____

_____

_____

- My favorite verse from Psalm 104:

  _____

  _____

  _____

- My favorite verse from Psalm 105:

  _____

  _____

  _____

Five points to ponder.

- Psalm 101 declares, (after a few Psalms beginning with the instructions to sing to the Lord) I will sing! May we be so obedient in living out the instructions within the Word. It's less about knowing more, but rather just doing more with what you know, wouldn't you say?!! The psalmist declares he will sing about God's love. No matter what, if, or when life throws us a curve ball we can always choose to sing of God's love, because of the cross AND His resurrection. We have eternal salvation because of His great love! This psalmist also makes clear he is drawing a hard line in the sand to honor God in a world that does not. How much are we tolerating things that dishonor our God? What kind of music do we listen to? Are the lyrics honoring the One who died to save you from vulgarness? What do we watch on T.V. are the story lines and characters aligning to Christ honoring material? Why would we tolerate anything that Jesus died to save us from?!

- Psalm 102 reveals a very discouraged person and yet they are leaning on God through prayer. It is often in our weakness that we find His greatest strength (see 2 Corinthians 12:9). What is it that turns this psalmist's eyes up? What brings him hope? What turns his tune? Verses 12-17. But God reigns and is coming back. This perspective frames discouragement and affliction in the brighter light of Living Hope! *Praise be to the God and Father of our Lord Jesus Christ! In his great mercy he has given us new birth into a living hope through the resurrection of Jesus Christ from the dead, 1 Peter 1:3 (NIV)*

- Psalm 103 is another Psalm I feel we could spend the whole of our 31 days on and still have more to discuss and savor! First, in verse 12 aren't you as glad as I that God didn't say as far as the north is from the south?! If I walk long enough from the south pole I'll eventually run into the north pole! God graciously removes our sin as far as the east is from the west. We can walk east and never meet the west unless we turn around and faith, my dear friend, always moves forward. Verse 2 reminds us not to forget. Forgetting God's faithfulness is a sure way to fall backwards in our faith journey. Keeping a prayer journal helps keep record of all the ways God has answered prayer and revealed His faithful presence in your life. That way you do have something personal, aside from all the pages of Scripture, that prove His faithfulness throughout the ages to look back on and jog your memory if ever you feel you've forgotten. I'm grateful in verse three God says He forgives ALL or sin and not just some. Verse 10 reminds us that He does not treat us as our sin deserves. True. We all deserve hell and Jesus, won us Heaven through His sacrifice! So if we get nothing else, if nothing else in life goes our way, we still have something to praise Him for and to be grateful about!! Verse four tells me that God doesn't pull me from the pit and say I told you so, but rather crowns me with love and compassion!!! How well am I doing at giving such a lavish gift, first given so freely to me, away to someone else?

- Psalm 104:24 reminds us that all of creation was by design. YOU are by design. Created in the wisdom and forethought of God Himself! Verse 28 reminds us that in just God's hand He is able to provide the sustenance for all things living! Verse 29, your very breath is a purposeful gift from God Almighty! No one else can gift you the breath of life! Verse 30, by His Spirit you have life, new life!! *For in him we live and move and have our being.' … Acts 17:28 (NIV) Jesus answered, "Very truly I tell you, no one can enter the kingdom of God unless they are born of water and the Spirit. John 3:5 (NIV)* It's not by being good enough that we get into the Kingdom of Heaven. We cannot be good enough. If we could have, then Jesus wouldn't have needed to do what He did (see Isaiah 59). We are born again upon receiving the Holy Spirit as a gift inside us once we confess our belief in Jesus as our personal Savior. *If you declare with your mouth, "Jesus is Lord," and believe in your heart that God raised him from the dead, you will be saved. Romans 10:9 (NIV)*

- Psalm 105:4 is one of my favorites. This verse beckons us to seek Him wholeheartedly as He holds the whole of our sustaining strength! This Psalm suggests a wonderful way to find Him as it recounts history recorded in the Bible. Search for Him in the pages of Scripture and we are sure to find Him. We will find Him to be unfailing love, faithful, reliable, good, gracious and full of mercy. We will find Him to be the great I AM, always enough. Romans 2:11 tells us God does not show favoritism. So as God led them day and night (verse 39) He will lead and guide us along the right paths (Psalm 23:3). As He provided sustenance, manna from heaven (verse 40) He is our Bread of Life (John 6:35). As He provided for life, refreshment in the wilderness (verse 41) Our Rock was split on the cross that we might have the living water welling up within us to eternal life (John 4:14). He did all of this with joy (verse 43) and we have the astounding Truth in Zephaniah 3:17 (NIV)! *The LORD your God is with you, the Mighty Warrior who saves. He will take great delight in you; in his love he will no longer rebuke you, but will rejoice over you with singing."* You are loved dearly by the One who beckons you to seek His face within the pages of Scripture showing His eyes to be brimming with compassionate strength that sustains through every mountain top and wilderness valley both night and day.

"Cool Down": Please record the coolest new thing God revealed to you this day.

_____

_____

_____

_____

_____

_____

_____

God bless you muchly~

~ DAY 22 ~

Date: _____

Hi! I'm so glad you are here. I find my mind marinating in yesterdays study of the Psalms. At the end of Psalm 105 in verse 44 (NIV) it states, *he gave them the lands of the nations, and they fell heir to what others had toiled for* - Now check out Exodus 23:28-31. Did you notice in verse 30 that God was going to remove the enemy little by little?! I wonder if there was anyone in that listening crowd that may have been a little like me wondering, why little by little God, can You just please take the enemy out quickly?! God, in His infinite wisdom had the enemy doing a job for His people!! If He had taken the enemy out quickly the Israelites would have been left with too much to handle so while the Israelites grew, God allowed the enemy to remain for a time (ultimately for His peoples good). By Psalm 105:44 we see that waiting on the Lord, submitting their ways to Him, granted more blessing then they could have ever imagined or ever produced for themselves if they had pushed their own agenda! I pray we desire, submit and trust His agenda for our lives today dear one.

Warm Up and Worship:

_____

_____

Pray Scripture: *May my meditation be pleasing to him, as I rejoice in the LORD. Psalm 104:34 (NIV)* Please continue in prayer as you prepare your heart and mind to meet with God Almighty.

P.R. & P.R.

_____

_____

_____

_____

_____

_____

_____

_____

_____

_____

Daily Devotional Reading: "A Game Changer"

But you will receive power when the Holy Spirit comes on you; and you will be my witnesses in Jerusalem, and in all Judea and Samaria, and to the ends of the earth." Acts 1:8 (NIV)

Take note of the word "and", right after the word "Jerusalem", in the above verse. This verse or Word was spoken by Jesus to those in Jerusalem, not America. The reason I'm a believer is because those that received Jesus' Word that day, before He ascended into heaven, were faithful. They didn't look at God's Word as merely a suggestion to do or not do as they felt like it. They took God's Word as Authoritative Truth, living their lives out according to it - and I'm saved (Romans 10:17)!

What Word has God given you today? By the power of His Holy Spirit within you as a believer, you have what it takes to carry it forth. You never know whose life might change for the better, forever, because you were faithful. Today, step forward into becoming the game changer He designed you to be.

I can do all things through Christ who strengthens me. Philippians 4:13 (NKJV)

~~~

Study in the Psalms: Today we will be reading Psalms 106, 107, 108, 109 and 110.

- Converse with God as you read through each Psalm.
- Pause and reflect on verses that catch your heart's attention.
- Record one verse from each Psalm that holds impact for you.
- Review your list. Is there a theme in the verses you highlighted? Take time and listen for God's voice to your heart.

- My favorite verse from Psalm 106:

_____

_____

_____

- My favorite verse from Psalm 107:

_____

_____

_____

- My favorite verse from Psalm 108:

  _____

  _____

  _____

- My favorite verse from Psalm 109:

  _____

  _____

  _____

- My favorite verse from Psalm 110:

  _____

  _____

  _____

Five points to ponder.

- Psalm 106 finds a praise formed following a miracle. I wonder how blessed God's heart would be if we praised before we saw the miracle?! In verse 14 we find the people giving in to the desires of the flesh within the desert wilderness. When we find ourselves in the "desert wilderness" seasons of life and the devil thinks it's prime time to devour us - don't give in! _1 Corinthians 16:13-14 (NIV) Be on your guard; stand firm in the faith; be courageous; be strong. Do everything in love. 1 Peter 5:8 (NIV) Be alert and of sober mind. Your enemy the devil prowls around like a roaring lion looking for someone to devour._ We see in verses 16-17 that the focus was off God and on self. They got swallowed up by self consumption! When our focus is consumed with God we don't ever have to worry about self because we know and trust God has us. Verse 20 warns us of the great exchange! It seems crazy to read these verses about idol worship however idols are are around every corner in our own world. Look at your calendar and see where you prioritize your time. Anything above God is misplaced worship and as verse 36 tells us it will become a snare to our flourishing as God, our Creator, intended. Verse 25 speaks of a grumbling attitude and when we forget Who our God is we become gloomy and grumbly too (Romans 1:21)! Verse 28 along with 2 Corinthians 6:14 warns us about yoking with the wrong crowd! *Do not be misled: "Bad company corrupts good character." 1 Corinthians 15:33 (NIV)* (See also Matthew 11:28-29) Psalm 106:43-45 is astounding!! We fail and God is constantly faithful (2 Timothy 2:13). The doxology of this book 4 of Psalms found in verse 48 mirrors the first Psalm of the book (Psalm 90:1-2)! From everlasting to everlasting He is faithful, praise Him!!

- Psalm 107 opens book 5 of the Psalms groupings. This final book includes Psalm 107-150. Psalm 107 is for sure a song to praise our Redeemer King! This Psalm speaks of four different types of distress and God's rescue therein. God rescues wanderers, prisoners, the distressed and the storm wrecked. Verse 20 (NIV) gets me. *He sent out his word and healed them; he rescued them from the grave.* He sent out His Word. *For the word of God is alive and active. Sharper than any double-edged sword, it penetrates even to dividing soul and spirit, joints and marrow; it judges the thoughts and attitudes of the heart. Hebrews 4:12 (NIV) so is my word that goes out from my mouth: It will not return to me empty, but will accomplish what I desire and achieve the purpose for which I sent it. Isaiah 55:11 (NIV) If I say, "I will not mention his word or speak anymore in his name," his word is in my heart like a fire, a fire shut up in my bones. I am weary of holding it in; indeed, I cannot. Jeremiah 20:9 (NIV)* Who have you shared God's healing Word with today?!

- Psalm 108 is a combination of Psalm 57:7-11 and Psalm 60:5-12. Why would that be? Isn't it a good thing to be reminded from time to time of things we THINK we already know?!! As a parent we also know this fact to be true with our children right?!! Our eternally perfect Parent, our Heavenly Father, knows a little repetition, a little friendly reminder never hurt anyone. Psalm 108:12-13 stands out to me in that the prayer is not for survival but for victory! Don't let the size of your mountain diminish your hope but rather embolden your confidence in the enormity of your God who is above every mountain! In our distress let's look for ways God is able to display His victorious strength (see 2 Corinthians 12:9).

- Psalm 109 shows us a man wronged and yet remains a man of prayer and a man who defaults to God's authority and ability to handle his enemies. *Cast your anxiety on him because he cares for you. 1 Peter 5:7 (NIV)* God sees it all, nothing escapes His notice (see Matthew 6:4, Genesis 16:13). *Blessed are those who mourn, for they will be comforted. Matthew 5:4 (NIV) For our struggle is not against flesh and blood, but against the rulers, against the authorities, against the spiritual forces of evil in the heavenly realms. Ephesians 6:12 (NIV)* The battle is beyond us but with God behind us and before us we can win every time!

- Psalm 110 speaks of our mighty and victorious Messiah, King of kings and great High Priest! *He who testifies to these things says, "Yes, I am coming soon." Amen. Come, Lord Jesus. Revelation 22:20 (NIV)*

"Cool Down": Record how God more clearly revealed His character to you today.

_____

_____

_____

_____

_____

_____

_____

God bless you muchly dear one~

Fit To Flourish

~ DAY 23 ~

Date: _____

Welcome dear one, I've been praying for you. I'm trusting God to lead each one of us into an encounter with Him as we prayerfully remain open to His leadership throughout our study.

I'm reminded of the story of Zacchaeus in Luke 19:1-10. The same Zacchaeus that children still today, sing the song about! You may know it, it goes something like this…

"Zacchaeus was a wee little man, a wee little man was he!
He climbed up in a sycamore tree, for the Lord he wanted to see!
And as the Savior passed that way He looked up in that tree…
And He said, 'Zaccaeus, you come down, for I'm going to your house today,
I'm going to your house today!'"

I wonder if in heaven Zacchaeus has asked the Lord if He might be willing to just change those lyrics a bit… as I'm not sure how many men would choose the description "a wee little man" as something to be identified by for centuries!! However I'm kinda glad Zacchaeus' short coming (literally and figuratively) is recorded in the Bible. Zacchaeus did not let what he fell "short" in, to keep him from encountering Jesus; neither should we. Let's begin!

Warm Up and Worship:

_____

_____

Pray Scripture: *My heart has heard you say, "Come and talk with me." And my heart responds, "LORD, I am coming." Psalm 27:1 (NLT)* Please continue in prayer as you prepare your heart and mind to meet with your Protector and Provider.

P.R. & P.R.

_____

_____

_____

_____

_____

_____

_____

_____

_____

_____

Daily Devotional Reading: "Winning"

In Jesus, you are always winning more than you are losing; in spite of how you feel or how things may appear.

When Moses was struggling with God's commission for him (Exodus 3, 4), God didn't build up his self esteem saying, but Moses you have been to the palace, you even know how to speak Egyptian… No! God, instead tells Moses, I chose you, I made you, I will be with you. … Because when our confidence is in Him, and our trust is in His Word, we become more than conquerors!

John 16:33 (NIV) "I have told you these things, so that in me you may have peace. In this world you will have trouble. But take heart! I have overcome the world."

Deuteronomy 20:4 (NIV) For the LORD your God is the one who goes with you to fight for you against your enemies to give you victory."

Romans 8:37 (NIV) No, in all these things we are more than conquerors through him who loved us.

~~~

Study in the Psalms: Today we will be reading Psalms 111, 112, 113, 114 and 115.

- Converse with God as you read through each Psalm.
- Pause and reflect on verses that catch your heart's attention.
- Record one verse from each Psalm that holds impact for you.
- Review your list. Is there a theme in the verses you highlighted? Take time and listen for God's voice to your heart.

- My favorite verse from Psalm 111:

_____

_____

- My favorite verse from Psalm 112:

_____

_____

- My favorite verse from Psalm 113:

  _____

  _____

- My favorite verse from Psalm 114:

  _____

  _____

- My favorite verse from Psalm 115:

  _____

  _____

Five points to ponder.

- So much of who God is, is revealed in this Psalm 111. He is righteous, glorious, majestic, gracious, compassionate, provider, mindful, trustworthy, faithful, powerful, just, eternal, redeemer, holy and awesome!! Yes, to Him does belong eternal praise (see verse 10)!! Verse 10 also states that the fear of God is the beginning of wisdom. When we are consumed with wholehearted worship of our God in sincerity and truth, we will have a heart full of reverent fear. When we want only to please Him, our lives will navigate wisely.

- Why do you think T.V. calls it "Breaking News"? Because all it usually does it break you right?!! But those of us in Christ have the eternal Good News that can never be rained on! *They will have no fear of bad news; their hearts are steadfast, trusting in the LORD. Their hearts are secure, they will have no fear; in the end they will look in triumph on their foes. Psalm 112:7-8 (NIV)* When we fear God we can live fearlessly!

- Psalm 113 reminds me that God does not see as the world sees. … *The LORD does not look at the things people look at. People look at the outward appearance, but the LORD looks at the heart." 1 Samuel 16:7 (NIV)* How can we be more intentional with seeing others as God sees them? I know one way is to pray for people. *But I tell you, love your enemies and pray for those who persecute you, Matthew 5:44 (NIV)* Probably before your prayers change them, they will begin to change you. Through prayer, fellowship with our Heavenly Father, He can transform our hearts to look more like His Son's. We want what breaks His heart, to break ours. *When he saw the crowds, he had compassion on them, because they were harassed and helpless, like sheep without a shepherd. Matthew 9:36 (NIV)*

- Psalm 114 is a reminder of God's awesomeness! He reigns and rules over all. He can part the sea to set people free (verse 3) and He can keep it together that He might walk on it to calm His loved ones in a storm (see Matthew 14:25)! Our God is the same yesterday, today and forever and He shows no favoritism (Hebrews 13:8, Romans 2:11)! Psalm 114:8 closes with a reminder of how Jesus provided the means of salvation. He our Rock and on the cross He was broken and from His side poured water and blood. We are washed by His Word covered by His redeeming blood and through faith, by grace we are saved!

- Psalm 115:1 reminds me of when John the Baptist spoke in *John 3:30 (NIV) He must become greater; I must become less."* A prayer of my heart (that needs prayer for courage even before praying it), is something like, whatever it may mean, may You be seen. Seen in my stewardship, reaction, response… Can you think of someone that has magnified the character of Christ in your life? I wonder if you've told them so. *I thank my God every time I remember you. Philippians 1:3 (NIV)* Psalm 115:16 reminds us the earth was given to us, and yet we broke it with our sin. But praise Jesus He has redeemed the deed and will return to make it all as it should be! *"But about that day or hour no one knows, not even the angels in heaven, nor the Son, but only the Father. … "Therefore keep watch, because you do not know on what day your Lord will come. Matthew 24:36,42 (NIV)* While we wait we can praise Him for what He has done, is doing and will do, for this side of Heaven will be the only time we can choose to worship through the sacrifice of praise in faith. For the day is coming when our faith will be made sight!

"Cool Down":

_____

_____

_____

_____

_____

_____

_____

Thank you sincerely for your perseverance in His Word with me dear one. His Word is our sustenance, our Bread of Life. *But solid food is for the mature, who by constant use have trained themselves to distinguish good from evil. Hebrews 5:14 (NIV)*

~ DAY 24 ~

Date: _____

Welcome I hope you are filled with peace, the Prince of Peace, as you join me today. Did you know that the Greek word for 'hope' is 'elpis' and is pronounced 'el-pece'. How great is that?! Hope is quite literally pronounced peace!! But it's so true, that when we hang our hope on Jesus, we do have peace! He is our Living Hope, our Prince of Peace (1 Peter 1:3, Isaiah 9:6, Ephesians 2:14) in every season! That's a reason to worship!

Warm Up and Worship:

_____

_____

Pray Scripture: *Rejoice always, pray continually, give thanks in all circumstances; for this is God's will for you in Christ Jesus. 1 Thessalonians 5:16-18 (NIV)* Dear Heavenly Father, thank You that we always have a reason to rejoice in You. Please give us Your strength and the will to receive and apply it to aligning our lives to living out Your perfect will. … Please continue in prayer as you prepare your heart and mind to meet with our ever present Prince of Peace.

P.R. & P.R.

_____

_____

_____

_____

_____

_____

_____

_____

_____

Daily Devotional Reading: "THE LORD IS THERE" (Ezekiel. 48:35)

...Their leaves will not wither, nor will their fruit fail. Every month they will bear fruit, because the water from the sanctuary flows to them....
Ezekiel 47:12 (NIV)

Wise advice my dad always gave me in times I struggled with anything from math homework to real life dilemmas was, "Go back to what you know and work forward from there." As we navigate this broken world where things are often unexplainable and the loud cry of "WHY?!" within our hearts seems to go unanswered, I find my dad's advice to ring true even still today.

And because of his glory and excellence, he has given us great and precious promises. These are the promises that enable you to share his divine nature and escape the world's corruption caused by human desires. 2 Peter 1:4 (NLT) *For no matter how many promises God has made, they are "Yes" in Christ. And so through him the "Amen" is spoken by us to the glory of God.* 2 Corinthians 1:20 (NIV) Is your life speaking a confident "Yes!" in the promises of God or a shaky "I'm not so sure?!"

Go back to the Truth you know in God's Word. Instead of worrying about what or how He WILL do things for you, stand firm on what Jesus has ALREADY done for you! His display of love on the cross and His power at the resurrection has won you victory over all the unknowns of this present life (John 16:33, 1 Corinthians 2:9)!

The promise written above from Ezekiel 47:12 reveals an Almighty reversal. A quick comparison of Amos 4:6-11 to Amos 9:13-15 paints a vivid picture of this reversal for us. Not because any of us deserves anything good (Romans 3:10, 23) but because our God IS good! God chose to become the sacrifice for our sin, rising again victorious over all that would threaten to entangle us from becoming the vessel of His victory He intended us to be! All the "why's?!" that threaten to tailspin us into darkness have been overcome by the Champion of heaven (John 1:5)!

We serve an infinite God that won us eternal life in paradise. We can in no way comprehend that with our finite minds anymore than we can comprehend the answer to many of our "why's?!" this side of heaven; even if He were to answer them plainly for us! The answer to receiving His gift of peace that passes understanding (Ephesians 2:14, John 14:27), which will take a transformation, a renewing of our minds (Romans 12:2), comes as you go back to the Truth you know. Go back to what you know to find your faith in all that you do not.

The promise spoken in Ezekiel of the Old Testament is repeated in Revelation 22:2 (NIV) of the New Testament, for God's Word never fails (Luke 1:37). The promise speaks of healing and continuous prosperity, and WHY?! Verse 3, ...*The throne of God and of the Lamb will be in the city*... His living water flows as it flows by His Spirit to our hearts (John 4:14) to rebuild, replant, restore and make new, even now, so we can take up hope and trust in all our "even if's..." this side of heaven, for God is with you... even there, dear one (1 Corinthians 13:12).

Because of God's tender mercy, the morning light from heaven is about to break upon us, to give light to those who sit in darkness and in the shadow of death, and to guide us to the path of peace. Luke 1:78-79 (NLT) See also Isaiah 61.

~~~

Study in the Psalms: Today we will be reading Psalms 116, 117, 118, 120 and 121. *Psalm 119 is the longest chapter in the Bible, complete with 176 verses!! That has earned it, it's own day of study, so we will circle back to Psalm 119 on day 31. You won't want to miss it for sure!!!!

- Converse with God as you read through each Psalm.
- Pause and reflect on verses that catch your heart's attention.
- Record one verse from each Psalm that holds impact for you.
- Review your list. Is there a theme in the verses you highlighted? Take time and listen for God's voice to your heart.

- My favorite verse from Psalm 116:

  _____

  _____

- My favorite verse from Psalm 117:

  _____

  _____

- My favorite verse from Psalm 118:

  _____

  _____

- My favorite verse from Psalm 120:

  _____

  _____

- My favorite verse from Psalm 121:

  _____

  _____

Five points to ponder.

- Psalm 116:1 begins with an expression of love to God. We can say I love You because… and list a thousand plus reasons for our love of Him. _We love because he first loved us. 1 John 4:19 (NIV)_ However God's love note back could just be I love you (period). Check out

Deuteronomy 7:6-8. He just loved us because He IS love, not because we did anything lovable first. In fact, *But God demonstrates his own love for us in this: While we were still sinners, Christ died for us. Romans 5:8 (NIV)* His love for us is based on Himself, who He is not on us or anything we did or could do. Isn't that freeing!! We can just rest in His unfailing love and from that place of lavish love we love Him back. *Psalm 116:10 (NLT) I believed in you, so I said,* ... This is quoted by Paul in *2 Corinthians 4:13 (NLT) But we continue to preach because we have the same kind of faith the psalmist had when he said, "I believed in God, so I spoke."* Paul goes on in verse 14, *We know that God, who raised the Lord Jesus, will also raise us with Jesus and present us to himself together with you.* Paul's, the psalmists, our faith too is based on Living Hope, our living God who keeps His promises. Psalm 116:15 reminds us that God carefully chooses the time we enter into His presence (See Matthew 10:29 and Psalm 139:16). This psalmist is very grateful for having been delivered from his affliction (verse 8) and thus states three things he will do to honor God. All three are things we too can do. First Psalm 116:13 talks of lifting the cup of salvation, we too can in the act of communion remember the cost of our salvation and honor Him reverently. Psalm 116:14 talks of keeping his vows, we too can keep our promises to God and live according to His Word. Psalm 116:17 talks of offering a sacrifice of praise, we too can choose to worship, to praise, even when we expect God to move right and instead He seems to take a left; because every left ends in an ultimate right for us in God's hand (see Romans 8:28).

- Psalm 117 gives two reasons to praise Him. When we need to offer a sacrifice of praise, when it seems especially hard to find a reason to praise, here are two steadfast reasons to lift our hearts to Him in wholehearted worship. One: His unfailing love. Two: His eternal faithfulness. If we never get anything else, this is more than enough. His heart is for everyone, all the nations, always has been and always will be. *After this I looked, and there before me was a great multitude that no one could count, from every nation, tribe, people and language, standing before the throne and before the Lamb. They were wearing white robes and were holding palm branches in their hands. And they cried out in a loud voice: "Salvation belongs to our God, who sits on the throne, and to the Lamb." All the angels were standing around the throne and around the elders and their living creatures. They fell down on their faces before the throne and worshiped God, saying: "Amen! Praise and glory and wisdom and thanks and honor and power and strength be to our God for ever and ever. Amen!" Revelation 7:8-12 (NIV)*

- Psalm 118:24 is a reminder that God has given you this day to LIVE and be glad. One of my all time favorite movies is "Pollyanna". Pollyanna makes up this game called the "Glad game" and it ends up changing the whole town as they look for the good in all things. We will find what we look for, whether it's an excuse, the negative, or the positive, you will find it. What are you looking for in your situations and in the people around you today? Psalm 118:22 is quoted by Jesus in Matthew 21:42 in reference to many that rejected Him and yet He would still be the foundational cornerstone of the new building - the Church. We see this Scripture also in Acts and 1 Peter. *For Jesus is the one referred to in the Scriptures, where it says, 'The stone that you builders rejected has now become the cornerstone.' There is salvation in no one else! God has given no other name under heaven by which we must be saved." Acts 4:11-12 (NLT) You are coming to Christ, who is the living cornerstone of God's temple. He was rejected by people, but chosen by God for great honor. ... As the Scriptures say, "I am placing a cornerstone in Jerusalem, chosen for great honor, and anyone who trusts in him will never be disgraced." Yes, you who trust him recognize the honor God has given him. But for those who reject him, "The stone that the builders rejected has now become the cornerstone." And, "He is the stone that makes people stumble, the rock that makes them fall." They stumble because they do not obey God's word, and so they meet the fate that was planned for them. 1 Peter 2:4,6-8 (NLT)*

- We are jumping over Psalm 119 for now as we said earlier, so let's move to Psalm 120. Psalms 120-134 are known as "songs of ascent". They were sung by the Jews as they made their pilgrimage to Jerusalem for the festivals. Psalm 120 sounds like they are far from other believers and are growing weary of that strain. As we head to church do you too have a sense of excitement to be joining those who are like minded in the faith?! There is encouragement, a sort of recharge that happens when believers gather together in worship! (See Hebrews 3:13) *And let us not neglect our meeting together, as some people do, but encourage one another, especially now that the day of his return is drawing near. Hebrews 10:25 (NLT)* Psalm 120:1 (NLT) begins, *I took my troubles to the LORD...* How often is the Lord our first go-to in our distress? Isaiah 9:6 tells us

He is our Wonderful Counselor, and dear one, He is always open and free of charge. We won't find another, more wise, caring or loving than He. We won't find anyone who understands the depths of our heart like He does for He knit it together!! So why is He so often the last one on our list or the one we spend the least amount of time with? This Psalm ends with longing for peace. *Blessed are the peacemakers, for they will be called children of God. Matthew 5:9 (NIV)* Too often we want to fight for peace which means there will be a battle and that indicates one winner and one loser. Doing things God's way, making peace, suggests there could be two winners. Humility is often the most important ingredient in making peace. *Peacemakers who sow in peace reap a harvest of righteousness. James 3:18 (NIV)*

- *Psalm 121:3 (NIV) He will not let your foot slip - he who watches over you will not slumber;* I love that! God doesn't sleep dear one so we can!!! We do not need to endure restless sleepless nights as if staying up would really help anything anyway! We can rest in the arms of the One who promises to keep watch without getting drowsy!! We will never outgrow our need for our Heavenly Father's watchful care and in this Psalm He promises it will always be there. Often I can let my problems get out of proportion because I've allowed my perspective of my God to get small. Look up, look up and seek His face and His strength continually (Psalm 105:4). He will always be bigger than what you face, always. *This is what the Sovereign LORD, the Holy One of Israel, says: "In repentance and rest is your salvation, in quietness and trust is your strength, but you would have none of it. Isaiah 30:15 (NIV)* Let's chose to be ones that take part in Who He is and what He freely offers dear one.

"Cool Down": Record what has filled you with His peace.

_____

_____

_____

_____

_____

_____

_____

Thank you dearly~

For he himself is our peace ... Ephesians 2:14 (NIV)

~ DAY 25 ~

Date: _____

Hi! I'm so glad you are here. I tried my hand at making hash browns this morning... why is something that looks and sounds so simple sometimes so impossible!! The only thing browning in my hash was my pan! Anyway, I'm grateful for the good graces of my patient family, for second chances, additional pans and SOS pads! In the end (that came maybe longer than anticipated) we did enjoy golden hash browns! It's the little things...

Warm Up and Worship:

_____
_____

Pray Scripture: *LORD, I wait for you; you will answer, Lord my God. Psalm 38:15 (NIV)* Please continue in prayer as you prepare your heart and mind to meet with the great I AM.

P.R. & P.R.

_____
_____
_____
_____
_____
_____
_____
_____

_____

_____

_____

Daily Devotional Reading: "A Candle Of Contrast"

…Can anything good come from there?"… "Come and see,"…
John 1:46 (NIV)

How often do preconceived notions keep us from life's greatest adventures? I guess, if we think about it we can't really know the answer to that question. John 1 holds a beautiful example of living the adventure, that could have been completely missed if they had given into preconceived notions.

John 1:40 tells us Andrew heard a word about Jesus AND acted upon that word to go and follow Jesus! John 1:41 tells us the first thing Andrew does upon following Jesus, is to find his brother AND tell him the word. *But if I say, "I will not mention his word or speak anymore in his name," his word is in my heart like a fire, a fire shut up in my bones. I am weary of holding it in; indeed, I cannot. Jeremiah 20:9 (NIV)* Andrew doesn't stop at just the hearing or the going or the sharing of the word, Andrew brings others to Jesus (John 1:42)!

Do our lives listen to the Word in a way that produces follow through/action on what we have heard?

Do our lives present an invitation that is attractive to the outside world to come and see, to experience the Living Hope and joy we have that supersedes our situation and circumstances?

Do our lives hold up a candle of contrast to the world's way? *"I am leaving you with a gift-- peace of mind and heart. And the peace I give is a gift the world cannot give. So do not be troubled or afraid. John 14:27 (NLT)*

Often our doubts, fears and preconceived notions hold us back from life's grand adventures... we ask, ... *Can anything good come from there?"* ... *John 1:46 (NIV)* Can anything good come from there, here, me, them, that... ?! Dear one, if you hear nothing else today hear this...

Jesus said to her, "I am the resurrection and the life. The one who believes in me will live, even though they die; and whoever lives by believing in me will never die. Do you believe this?" John 11:25-26 (NIV) Therefore, my dear brothers and sisters, stand firm. Let nothing move you. Always give yourselves fully to the work of the Lord, because you know that your labor in the Lord is not in vain. 1 Corinthians 15:58 (NIV) He said to them, "Go into all the world and preach the gospel to all creation. Mark 16:15 (NIV) so is my word that goes out from my mouth: It will not return to me empty, but will accomplish what I desire and achieve the purpose for which I sent it. Isaiah 55:11 (NIV)

Come and see dear one, come see and experience the Word, for you were built to be a candle of contrast in this world; reflecting the Light and love of Jesus! *For we are God's masterpiece. He has created us anew in Christ Jesus, so that we can do the good things he planned for us long ago. Ephesians 2:10 (NLT) In the same way, let your light shine before others, that they may see your good deeds and glorify your Father in heaven. Matthew 5:16 (NIV)*

~~~

Study in the Psalms: Today we will be reading Psalms 122, 123, 124, 125 and 126.

- Converse with God as you read through each Psalm.
- Pause and reflect on verses that catch your heart's attention.
- Record one verse from each Psalm that holds impact for you.
- Review your list. Is there a theme in the verses you highlighted? Take time and listen for God's voice to your heart.

- My favorite verse from Psalm 122:

_____

_____

- My favorite verse from Psalm 123:

_____

_____

- My favorite verse from Psalm 124:

_____

_____

- My favorite verse from Psalm 125:

  _____

  _____

  _____

- My favorite verse from Psalm 126:

  _____

  _____

  _____

Five points to ponder.

- There is such a beautiful heart of worship displayed in Psalm 122. They are seeking peace, but the kind of peace that the world cannot give and only comes from God. *"I am leaving you with a gift - peace of mind and heart. And the peace I give is a gift the world cannot give. So don't be troubled or afraid. John 14:27 (NLT)* This is the kind of peace that flows from having peace with God. *Romans 5:1 (NIV) Therefore, since we have been justified through faith, we have peace with God through our Lord Jesus Christ,* Psalm 122:8 was the verse that most grabbed my attention as it reminded me of Isaiah 49:16 (NIV). *See, I have engraved you on the palms of my hands; your walls are ever before me.* I have this verse up on my wall next to the six hand prints of my children. I pray they always take up the gift of faith and that God Almighty dwells within their "walls". That they know in every fiber of their being that they are loved beyond imagination - a love engraved upon nail scared hands - unfailing and unfading and unfaltering forever and always no matter what. *For the sake of my family and friends, I will say, "Peace be within you." Psalm 122:8 (NIV) For he himself is our peace… Ephesians 2:14 (NIV)*

- Psalm 123 finds a people enduring intense ridicule from other people. Instead of retaliating on their own, taking matters in their own hands, they look up to God. Instead of looking inward and letting the lies and ridicule take root and discourage and depress them, they look up to God. They fix their gaze on the One above it all and keep it there. That is how we will hear the Truth whispered loudly within, sustaining us. I whisper becomes loud when our ear is pressed up against the whisperer. God wants us close, its the safest place to be, so look up and lean in and keep on dear one. *fixing our eyes on Jesus, the pioneer and perfecter of faith. For the joy set before him he endured the cross, scorning its shame, and sat down at the right hand of the throne of God. Consider him who endured such opposition from sinners, so that you will not grow weary and lose heart. Hebrews 12:2-3 (NIV)*

- Recently someone communicated to me that they could not believe God would use them considering their past. I thought, isn't that all of us though?! We could all relate to this Psalm 124 could we not?! It's why Jesus came to earth, to pay the penalty for our sin, ALL of our sins. *for all have sinned and fall short of the glory of God, Romans 3:23 (NIV) He saw that there was no one, he was appalled that there was no one to intervene; so his own arm achieved salvation for him, and his own righteousness sustained him. He put on righteousness as his breastplate, and the helmet of salvation on this head; he put on the garment of vengeance and wrapped himself in zeal as in a cloak. Isaiah 59:16-17 (NIV) But the angel said to them, "Do not be afraid. I bring you good news that will cause great joy for all the people. Luke 2:10 (NIV)* The fleeting envious thought brought Him to the cross just as much as the murderous one. Where would any of us be without Him? *do not consider yourself to be superior to those other branches. If you do, consider this: You do not support the root, but the root supports you. Romans 11:18 (NIV)* Not one of us would even have woken up this morning if He had not given us the breath to do so! So may none of us ever loose the wonder expressed in Psalm 124, for, *What if the LORD had not been on our side? … Psalm 124:1 (NLT) And having disarmed the powers and authorities, he made a public spectacle of them, triumphing over them by the cross. Colossians 2:15 (NIV)* Praise be to the God and Father *of our Lord Jesus Christ! In his great mercy he has given us new birth into a living hope through the resurrection of Jesus Christ form the dead, 1 Peter 1:3 (NIV)*

• We become like what we worship, we've made note of that already. So here in Psalm 125:1 when it states those who trust in God are unshakable it's true because our God is unshakably trustworthy! *"But blessed is the one who trusts in the LORD, whose confidence is in him. Jeremiah 17:7 (NIV)* Check out David's confident trust in God record in Psalm 18:1-2 (NIV). *I love you, Lord, my strength. The Lord is my rock, my fortress and my deliverer; my God is my rock, in whom I take refuge, my shield and the horn of my salvation, my stronghold.* That kind of confident trust develops over time as a relationship is built. This is why it's so important to be in God's Word daily! It's like brushing your teeth. You don't only brush your teeth when you have a cavity, you do it daily to prevent a cavity! The more we daily walk with God the more equipped we will be to remain steadfastly unshaken when bad things happen because we know Who holds our hand. Nothing we face will be bigger than He, nor have the ability to trump His promises. *For I am the Lord your God who takes hold of your right hand and says to you, Do not fear; I will help you. Isaiah 41:13 (NIV) …Lead me to the rock that is higher than I… Psalm 61:2 (ESV)*

- Psalm 126 reminds me of John 11:25-26 (NIV) *Jesus said to her, "I am the resurrection and the life. The one who believe in me will live, even thought hey die; and whoever lives by believing in me will never die. Do you believe this?"* God's ability to turn any and every situation around (even dead ones) is astounding! He is Living Hope! He reveals this truth in His creation… fall turns to spring, caterpillars become butterflies, broken bones heal, forests burned completely grow back… The key is how you answer the question in John 11:26… do you believe? (See also Mark 9:23) The key to how we answer that question is how we receive the seed of God's Word. (See Matthew 13:1-23) *For the word of God is alive and active. Sharper than any double-edged sword, it penetrates even to divided soul and spirit, joints and marrow; it judges the thoughts and attitudes of the heart. Hebrews 4:12 (NIV)* (See also 2 Timothy 3:16-17 and Isaiah 55:11)

"Cool Down": Record how God's Word has fallen afresh on your soul today dear one.

_____

_____

_____

_____

_____

_____

_____

Grace and Peace~

~ DAY 26 ~

Date: _____

Greetings! Let's get right down to business shall we?!

Warm Up and Worship: What makes you smile?

_____

_____

Pray Scripture: *Though the mountains be shaken and the hills be removed, yet my unfailing love for you will not be shaken nor my covenant of peace be removed,"* says the Lord, who has compassion on you. *Isaiah 54:10 (NIV)* Please continue in prayer as you prepare your heart and mind to meet with our Strength and Shield our Safe Place and Refuge.

P.R. & P.R.

_____

_____

_____

_____

_____

_____

_____

_____

_____

Daily Devotional Reading: "A Sure Hope"

Now hope does not disappoint, because the love of God has been poured out in our hearts by the Holy Spirit who has been given to us. Romans 5:5 (NKJV)

The word *hope* in Hebrew is *tiqva* and literally means *cord*. In Joshua 2 the prostitute Rahab throws a scarlet cord out her window in faith that the God of the Israelites would love even her, would save even her… and He does. When the mighty walls of Jericho fall in Joshua 6, the only spot in the wall still standing is none other than Rahab's house!!

The rain came down, the streams rose, and the winds blew and beat against that house; yet it did not fall, because it had its foundation on the rock. Matthew 7:25 (NIV) When we tie or anchor our hope to the Rock of Living Hope Himself (Ps. 18:1-2, 1 Pt. 1:3), our Immanuel (God with us in each step) our every step can be lived in unshaken confidence in the Word of God. *Though the mountains be shaken and the hills be removed, yet my unfailing love for you will not be shaken nor my covenant of peace be removed," says the LORD, who has compassion on you. Isaiah 54:10 (NIV)*

What or who are you tethering your hope to? If you are reading this it's not too late if you need to re-tie your cord of hope to the anchor of Living Hope dear one.

May the God of hope fill you with all joy and peace as you trust in him so that you may overflow with hope by the power of the Holy Spirit. Romans 15:13 (NIV)

Study in the Psalms: Today we will be reading Psalms 127, 128, 129, 130 and 131.

- Converse with God as you read through each Psalm.
- Pause and reflect on verses that catch your heart's attention.
- Record one verse from each Psalm that holds impact for you.
- Review your list. Is there a theme in the verses you highlighted? Take time and listen for God's voice to your heart.

- My favorite verse from Psalm 127:

_____

_____

_____

- My favorite verse from Psalm 128:

_____

_____

_____

- My favorite verse from Psalm 129:

_____

_____

_____

- My favorite verse from Psalm 130:

_____

_____

_____

- My favorite verse from Psalm 131:

_____

_____

_____

Five points to ponder.

- Psalm 127 reminds me of _Ecclesiastes 4:12 (NIV) Though one may be overpowered, two can defend themselves. A cord of three strands in not quickly broken._ Unless God builds the family, the relationships, even the business, we labor in vain, our efforts afford useless gain. Remember Psalm 37:3-5? This is the way we do Psalm 127. _Take delight in the LORD, and he will give you the desires of your heart. Commit your way to the LORD; trust in him and he will do this: Psalm 37:3-5 (NIV)_ Things may not always end up like you first pictured in your mind but when you roll your plans out at His feet and let Him build, He will give you a better picture framed in a greater perspective. Psalm 127:2 isn't encouraging laziness just as much as it isn't encouraging an excessive amount of endless work. This Psalm encourages a balance of trusting while you work but also resting in that trust. I appreciate that verse 4 compares children to arrows. To use an arrow correctly it takes skill, precision and practice. Not every arrow is the same depending on your activity. Shooting an arrow is nothing like throwing a rock, where any old "chuck it!" will do. Thus God compares children to arrows. Each one different by design and without their Creator's wisdom pouring through us as parents, we are utterly lost as to how to train them up in the way they should go! Only God can train your heart and mind to raise "arrows" for Him.

- Psalm 128 piggy backs onto Psalm 127. This Psalm states that the fruit of ones labor that has chosen to trust God's way and obey accordingly will be blessed. Let us not be deceived like Eve in Genesis 3. We do not know better than God - ever. *Trust in the LORD with all your heart and lean not on your own understanding; Proverbs 3:5 (NIV)*

- Psalm 129:2 states they have been greatly oppressed and yet, the enemy has not gained victory over them!! In Jesus we have this same promise! *We are hard pressed on every side, but not crushed; perplexed, but not in despair; persecuted, but not abandoned; struck down, but not destroyed. 2 Corinthians 4:8-9 (NIV)* (See also Romans 8:31-39) *The Lord will rescue me from every evil attack and will bring me safely to his heavenly kingdom. To him be glory for ever and ever. Amen. 2 Timothy 4:18 (NIV)* So… *Let us not become weary in doing good, for at the proper time we will reap a harvest if we do not give up. Galatians 6:9 (NIV)*

- Psalm 130:4 is packed full with life giving Truth that the enemy will combat at every turn! Dear one do not let the enemy get a foothold where this Truth sets you free!! *Psalm 130:4 (NIV) But with you there is forgiveness, so that we can, with reverence, serve you.* If you will please circle "so that we can". We are not only forgiven, which in itself is life giving!! But with forgiveness God still sees GREAT purpose for our lives!! He desires to set us free with the intention that we will get back in the game!! Too often we falter and fail and feel like we are only good for fodder and that's just what the enemy would like us to think. If the enemy can get you to believe you belong on the sidelines, on the bench, you've made his job easy! Take hold of Psalm 130:4 and other promises like *Micah 7:8 (NIV) Do not gloat over me, my enemy! Through I have fallen, I will rise. Through I sit in darkness, the Lord will be my light.* (See also how Jesus speaks to Peter in Luke 22:31-32.) We must do as Psalm 130:5 (NIV) directs, *…in his word I put my hope.* Put your hope in the steadfast Truth of His Word and all that God speaks over your life. You are valued, with great purpose, precious in His eyes dear one, don't ever, ever doubt it. You cannot wander so far His arm cannot save and redeem any failure. *Surely the arm of the LORD is not too short to save, nor his ear too dull to hear. Isaiah 59:1 (NIV) …for with the LORD is unfailing love and with him is full redemption. Psalm 130:7 (NIV)* Hope in our God will never disappoint (see Romans 5:5). Psalm 130:6 reminds me of the hope held in Lamentations 3:22-23. Every morning His mercies are new and fresh! 365 days, 365 new chances! Dear one though the night seems long, there is hope with the dawn… don't give up in the wait for it!!!!

- Psalm 131 is a reminder to me that when I let humility and trust in God frame my perspective I find rest and strength to serve Him and others. A nursing child fusses and cries for feeding time; a weaned child understands he will be fed and doesn't need to franticly fuss for fear of starvation! *This is what the Sovereign LORD, the Holy One of Israel, says: "In repentance and rest is your salvation, in quietness and trust is your strength, but you would have none of it. Isaiah 30:15 (NIV)* We have a choice over who's will we will fight for. We will always serve something whether it be self or something else. Let's choose to make our lives count for something bigger than self. *Humble yourselves, therefore, under God's mighty hand, that he may lift you up in due time. 1 Peter 5:6 (NIV)*

"Cool Down": What Truth can you rest in today?

_____

_____

_____

_____

_____

_____

_____

Shalom (Hebrew word for peace.)~

~ DAY 27 ~

Date: _____

Hello! I'm so glad you are here. I'm grateful that God has used the similar desire we both have to know Him more deeply, to intersect our paths. As much as we can learn from those similar to us, we can also learn much from those very different from us. We can learn from anyone no matter how good or bad the pairing is as long as we are open to what God is teaching us through it. It may be how NOT to be, or maybe how to BE more patient with differences, but we can ALWAYS learn something if we are humble, willing and flexible! Praise God He created the muscle with the ability to become more flexible with practice! *Romans 15:4 (NIV) For everything that was written in the past was written to teach us, so that through the endurance taught in the Scriptures and the encouragement they provide we might have hope.*

Warm Up and Worship:

_____

_____

Pray Scripture: *You make known to me the path of life; you will fill me with joy in your presence, with eternal pleasures at your right hand. Psalm 16:11 (NIV)* Please continue in prayer as you prepare your heart and mind to meet with our Living Hope.

P.R. & P.R.

_____

_____

_____

_____

_____

_____

_____

_____

_____

_____

Daily Devotional Reading: "Sweat Spot or Sweet Spot"

It was the perfect, on-the-verge-of-fall day! The wind was blustery and the air was crisp and cool. Twirl winds of leaves, just beginning to hint at changing colors from green to all sorts of fiery yellow, orange and red were cascading down the street that the wild wisps had managed to shake loose. This day I was able to work from home, so after dropping the herd off at the bus stop and blowing kisses to fly in the wind alongside the leaves, I headed home for the most important item on my to-do list: Bake homemade chocolate chip cookies for after school (of course). (How effective is working from home REALLY?? Especially when it's the PERFECT day for baking!)

Once home I got right to it. I practically know this recipe by heart, as I bake it ALL the time. It's my mom's recipe that she always used to bake for me growing up. Literally I've found none to compare in all my multiple decades of living, thus far. So in an effort to truly be productive and work efficiently I decided to skip reading the recipe… after-all I KNEW what to do, I could lean on my own understanding (or so I thought… famous last words right!?!).

Upon opening the oven I realized that in my perfect (not so perfect) memory of the recipe, I had mistaken the oven temperature setting to be 350 instead of 375! Really though, what does 25 degrees matter in the realm of 300-some anyway?!! I'll tell you what, those few degrees make the difference between a hot gooy gross total mess and a golden crisp outside with a soft center bit of perfection to die for! Again God sent His Scripture connection…

When I lean on my own understanding I often find myself a hot mess, in a sweat spot rather than in my sweet spot!

- Think of Johnathan, a good, kind, upstanding man and the next in line rightfully for the throne after his father Saul. YET God chose David to succeed Saul. Jonathan's response is to submit to God's choosing and encourage, support and fight FOR David!

- Think of David after becoming king, he has all the power, the resources and leadership skill to build the Temple for God, it's even his idea. YET God chose Solomon to build it. David responds with "Who am I, Sovereign LORD, and what is my family, that you have brought me this far? (2 Samuel 7:18) Total humility and submission to the Father's will and way.

- Think of Barnabas, a great man of encouragement and YET God chooses Paul to lead. When no one would give Saul (turned Paul) a chance, Barnabas didn't seize the moment to get ahead but rather to build a bridge for Paul to step into what Barnabas had seen God doing in his life.

- Think of Naomi, a woman of God and YET God chooses Ruth, her daughter in law from a pagan land to be the mother of king David's grandfather. Naomi takes Ruth under her wing and celebrates what God is doing in her DIL's life.

It's easy to get strung up on what we THINK we understand even though God's Word clearly advises otherwise (Isaiah 55:8-9)! I mean, where would David have been if Johnathan had not fought for him? Where would Solomon have been if David had not supported him? Where would Paul have been if Barnabas had not forged the bridge of acceptance for him? Where would Ruth have been if Naomi had not brought her into the family of God?

Regardless of what you THINK your life should look like right now, if you are abiding in Him don't sweat it! You have been given the leading role in your own life, step into it as God designed! Your script is God's bright idea! Whether you are called to submit like Johnathan, support like David, encourage like Barnabas, shepherd like Naomi… do it all to the glory of God! There are no small roles in HisStory, the Author of time and space does not waste it dear one! *Trust in the Lord with all your heart and lean not on your own understanding; in all your ways submit to him, and he will make your paths straight.* Proverbs 3:5-6 (NIV) This, dear one, will always be your sweet spot.

~~~

Study in the Psalms: Today we will be reading Psalms 132, 133, 134, 135 and 136.

- Converse with God as you read through each Psalm.
- Pause and reflect on verses that catch your heart's attention.
- Record one verse from each Psalm that holds impact for you.
- Review your list. Is there a theme in the verses you highlighted? Take time and listen for God's voice to your heart.

- My favorite verse from Psalm 132:

_____

_____

_____

- My favorite verse from Psalm 133:

_____

_____

_____

- My favorite verse from Psalm 134:

_____

_____

_____

- My favorite verse from Psalm 135:

  _____

  _____

  _____

- My favorite verse from Psalm 136:

  _____

  _____

  _____

Five points to ponder.

- Psalm 132 describes David's strong desire to, one; bring the Ark of
  the Covenant back to Jerusalem and two: build a Temple for God.
  (See 2 Samuel 6 and 7) The Ark was eventually restored to it's
  rightful place and this job of building a Temple ended up falling to
  his son Solomon via God's choosing. The first part of this Psalm
  indicates that David's whole being was consumed with
  implementing God's perfect will in His perfect way. I pray that I
  would walk so closely with God that He would make me restlessly
  consumed with aligning my life with His. When I say restlessly
  consumed I don't mean with a lack of peace because He is always
  Peace. Peace doesn't guarantee I won't have problems but that the
  problems won't have me. So my use of restlessly consumed just
  means that if God has pricked my heart with something
  specifically on His I would not rest until I have wrestled it into the
  clarity He would desire for me to perceive it. This requires an
  authentically close walk with Him and I pray I would make myself

available to Him to develop that with me. A good place to start in creating a welcoming place for Him would be to do as we do at the beginning of each day… worship and praise! Psalm 22:3 tells us God inhabits the praises of His people. The last two verses in Psalm 132 that refer to the increase in David's rule and reign through his descendants certainly holds true as Solomon was a very wise and influential king. However Jesus our Messiah also came through David's royal line and is the ultimate fulfillment of The Anointed One.

- Psalm 133 speaks of harmony amongst God's people. Why is that so important? It magnifies Him. *By this everyone will know that you are my disciples, if you love one another." John 13:35 (NIV)* While on earth Jesus prayed for it. *that all of them may be one, Father, just as you are in me and I am in you. May they also be in us so that the world may believe that you have sent me. John 17:21 (NIV) For he himself is our peace, who has made the two groups one and has destroyed the barrier, the dividing wall of hostility, Ephesians 2:14 (NIV)* Living in harmony with everyone is impossible apart from our IAMpossible God. *Now may the God of peace, who through the blood of the eternal covenant brought back from the dead our Lord Jesus, that great Shepherd of the sheep, equip you with everything good for doing his will, and may he work in us what is pleasing to him, through Jesus Christ, to whom be glory for ever and ever. Amen. Hebrews 13:20-21 (NIV)*

- Psalm 134 is about a small group of people doing their job of watching over the Temple day and night. It was seen as an act of praise. May all that we are and all that we do be in wholehearted devotion/service motivated by our Savior's lavish love for us, thus producing His praise in others. *Serve wholeheartedly, as if you were serving the Lord, not people, Ephesians 6:7 (NIV) This service that you perform is not only supplying the needs of the Lord's people but is also overflowing in many expressions of thanks to God. 2 Corinthians 9:12 (NIV)*

- Psalm 135 praises God and recounts His mighty acts and recalls His ultimate authority over all. It is good to be in His story daily so that we remember that His story not only includes us but is bigger than us. Romans 11:1-6 is a reminder to know the Scriptures and remember that God has not forgotten you, you are not alone. God is still on the throne and moving on His redemptive plan for all the world, which, dear one, includes you and me even when we cannot make sense of it all! So we must not measure His love and available power to us by our situation and circumstances. Rather remember and measure His love by the cross He endured to pay our debt and the empty tomb He conquered that we might live free for eternity! Don't give in to the temptation to take things into your own hands, to make idols out of ignorance. Choose to trust the Truth that says, *Keep your lives free from the love of money and be content with what you have, because God has said, "Never will I leave you; never will I forsake you." Hebrews 13:5 (NIV)*

- Psalm 136 repeats 26 times, "His faithful love endures forever." How would our day look different if we responded to everything that came at us, first and foremost, with the phrase, "His faithful love endures forever."? What if we framed everyone of our current circumstance with that thought?

"Cool Down": How have you experienced His enduring and faithful love for you?

_____

_____

_____

_____

_____

_____

_____

_____

His faithful love for you endures forever dear one.

~ DAY 28 ~

Date: _____

Hello! I'm so glad you were able to join me today. I'm especially grateful that we serve a God who is able even when I am not. *Now to him who is able to do immeasurably more than all we ask or imagine, according to his power that is at work within us, Ephesians 3:20 (NIV)* Our God IS able, nothing is too hard for Him. The more I get to know Him and His faithful Word the more I am able to receive His peace that passes understanding (Philippians 4:7) at the times I know He is able to do "a, b or c" and yet chooses not to. *The Lord is righteous in all his ways and faithful in all he does. Psalm 145:17 (NIV) He is the Rock, his works are perfect, and all his ways are just. A faithful God who does no wrong, upright and just is he. Deuteronomy 32:4 (NIV) Oh, the depths of the riches of the wisdom and knowledge of God! How unsearchable his judgments, and his paths beyond tracing out! Romans 11:33 (NIV)*

Warm Up and Worship:

_____

_____

Pray Scripture: *The Sovereign Lord has given me a well-instructed tongue, to know the word that sustains the weary. He wakens me morning by morning, wakens my ear to listen like one being instructed. Isaiah 50:4 (NIV)* Please continue in prayer as you prepare your heart and mind to meet with our Wisdom.

P.R. & P.R.

_____

_____

_____

_____

_____

_____

_____

_____

_____

Daily Devotional Reading: "Signpost Of Peace"

In the beginning God... Genesis 1:1 (NIV)

Signposts are everywhere. They can be on the side of the road or even found as literary elements in speech. Wherever you find them their purpose is the same; to eliminate the element of confusion. A state of confusion rarely emits feelings of serenity. In fact, quite the opposite. When you feel lost and confused feelings of fear and anxiety grow naturally and often out of proportion - quickly. If you have ever been to the ocean you know how important it is to stake out a visual signpost at the point you enter the water. If you don't, the tide and waves will take you far beyond where you started and it is easy to become disoriented and lost!

Life can be like the big unknown ocean, and although it holds incredible depths of beauty and adventure it also can be daunting, dark, dangerous and scary! This is why we need to recognize our sure, steady and strong, signpost of Peace. However it is not enough just to recognize Him, we must receive Him in so that we can stake our lives, our emotions, our circumstances and relationships to a Peace that passes understanding. *For he himself is our peace… Ephesians 2:14 (NIV) Do not be anxious about anything, but in every situation, by prayer and petition, with thanksgiving, present your requests to God. And the peace of God, which transcends all understanding, will guard your hearts and your minds in Christ Jesus. Philippians 4:6-7 (NIV)*

The Word of God begins with, *In the beginning God… Genesis 1:1 (NIV)* yet how often do we begin every moment with Jesus Christ as our first thought? How rooted are we to the sure reign and rule of our God?! We are given great and precious promises to root us unshaken in this world (2 Peter 1:4) all of which are confirmed authentic and true in Jesus Christ (2 Corinthians 1:20)! If we entered into every situation, EVERY one, with the Truth of Jesus FIRST, how would that change our lives? (See, Isaiah 26:3, Jeremiah 17:7-9)

For unto us a child is born, to us a son is given, and the government will be on his shoulders. And he will be called Wonderful Counselor, Mighty God, Everlasting Father, Prince of Peace. Isaiah 9:6 (NIV) How often do you think our God is huddling up the hosts of Heaven around the whiteboard, clipboard in hand, to re-run that earthly play wondering WHAT angel was on THAT play that totally botched!?!? NEVER!! Our God's eternal reign and rule over all is real (Colossians 1:17)! Even when things look like defeat it is still victory! Glance at

Genesis 45:4-9. Joseph portrays a perfect example on how to put God first, framing a victory out of what appeared at first like defeat! Don't let the wind and the waves over your ocean drown you in defeat because you stopped looking up to your signpost of Peace dear one. He is there, trustworthy and true, with hope like an anchor, firm and secure for your soul. *But thanks be to God! He gives us the victory through our Lord Jesus Christ. 1 Corinthians 15:57 (NIV)*

Today, begin with God. May your narrative today sound like, In the beginning God... Root your mind and heart around His promises and remember His steadfast rule and reign in and through all of your moments today and live set free to experience Peace; Peace that walks on the wind and waves of your ocean, until one day all storms cease, *that at the name of Jesus every knee should bow, in heaven and on earth and under the earth, and every tongue acknowledge that Jesus Christ is Lord, to the glory of God the Father. Philippians 2:10-11 (NIV)*

~~~

Study in the Psalms: Today we will be reading Psalms 137, 138, 139, 140 and 141.

- Converse with God as you read through each Psalm.
- Pause and reflect on verses that catch your heart's attention.
- Record one verse from each Psalm that holds impact for you.
- Review your list. Is there a theme in the verses you highlighted? Take time and listen for God's voice to your heart.

- My favorite verse from Psalm 137:

  _____

  _____

- My favorite verse from Psalm 138:

  _____

  _____

- My favorite verse from Psalm 139:

  _____

  _____

- My favorite verse from Psalm 140:

  _____

  _____

- My favorite verse from Psalm 141:

  _____

  _____

Five points to ponder.

- Psalm 137 is a song of lament. The Jews taken captive to Babylon cannot seem to find any song in their heart. Yet somehow upon their release 70 years later some have become so content in Babylon that they stay instead of head back to Jerusalem! (See the book of Esther which is about the ones who stayed behind.) Often we make allowances little by little, we tolerate more sin than we should until all of a sudden we look up and don't even recognize how we got so far down that road. The road of sin is often a slow fade but a slippery slope. The more we tolerate the more we become desensitized to that which is only here to steal, kill and destroy (John 10:10). I pray that God would embolden our desire for obedience thus producing perseverance in what is right. I pray that in a world that preaches tolerance we would not begin to sing along to the tune of captivity.

- *Psalm 138:8 (NLT) The LORD will work out his plans for my life- for your faithful love, O LORD, endures forever. Don't abandon me, for you made me.* He made us, we are His workmanship. *Ephesians 2:10 (ESV) For we are his workmanship, created in Christ Jesus for good works, which God prepared beforehand, that we should walk in them.* The Greek word for workmanship is poiema from which we get our word poem. Actually my computer even tries to auto correct the Greek word poiema to poem!! Dear one, we are God's poetry! Amazing! He is writing out our lives in such a way that we might be a display of His splendor! He will not forsake us! He bought us with His very life while we were dead in our sin! He has always valued us but that value is not based on us, but rather on Who He is! Psalm 138:2 reminds us how seriously He takes His Word to us. He has said in Philippians 1:6 that we can be confident that the good work He started in us, He will carry on to completion! Don't give up on Him dear one, He will not ever give up on you. Our next Psalm is continued confirmation of His enduring, unfailing and steadfast love for us.

- Psalm 139 reminds us in a posing world especially with social media and technology these days we can air brush anything posing and presenting only what we want people to see and know or think about us. Why? For fear if they knew or saw the real us they wouldn't like us or we wouldn't measure up maybe even for our own standards. It can be hard to even be real with ourselves at times!! How refreshing that we cannot "pose" before God. He knows us better that we know ourselves - the good, the bad and the ugly… and He loves us totally. It's so comforting to know we have a God that knows us better than we know ourselves. The One who knit our hearts together is our Wonderful Counselor! When we can't understand our feelings He alone can find the perfect healing. One of my favorite Scriptures to turn into prayer is Psalm 139:23-24 because I have One who can redirect before I know I'm off track. May I be one to take the time to ask and then to listen, following in obedience. Psalm 139:13-16 is a Truth I pray will always ring louder in your mind and heart than anything else the world may say about you. Remember Ehud from Judges 3?! He was born left handed and yet he was from the tribe of Benjamin which means - son of my right hand. I wonder how often he felt like a mistake… See Judges 3 and it was exactly the fact that Ehud was designed left handed that he became the victor!!! God knows what He is doing - trust Him who does not make mistakes. Psalm 139:17-18 reminds us of His precious thoughts about us, His love note containing these thoughts is often found in His Word! Jeremiah 29:11 reminds us His well thought out plans for our lives our good, hope filled and involve a future with Him, the One who loves us more than we could ever imagine! Who would we rather give our hearts more fully to than Him! *May you experience the love of Christ, though it is too great to understand fully. Then you will be made complete with all the fullness of life and power that comes from God. Ephesians 3:19 (NLT)*

- Psalm 140 depicts evil in pursuit. The devil wants what is valuable to God so we can count on evil being in pursuit of us as well. But for those of us in Jesus we have nothing to fear! *The Lord will rescue me from every evil attack and will bring me safely to his heavenly kingdom. To him be glory for ever and ever. Amen. 2 Timothy 4:18 (NIV)* When the enemies tactics cause us to press deeper into our God, into His Word, they contribute to our victory, our success!!! *That is why, for Christ's sake, I delight in weaknesses, in insults, in hardships, in persecutions, in difficulties. For when I am weak, then I am strong. 2 Corinthians 12:10 (NIV)* Psalm 140:4-5 (NIV) states, *Keep me safe, LORD, from the hands of the wicked; protect me from the violent, who devise ways to trip my feet. The arrogant have hidden a snare for me; they have spread out the cords of their net and have set traps for me along my path.* Now, like the end of this Psalm in verse 12, the psalmist remembers Truth. Let's remember and apply two fear dispelling Truths to Psalm 140:4-5. Number 1 is found in Jude 24 (NIV) *To him who is able to keep you from stumbling and to present you before his glorious presence without fault and with great joy-* No trap of the enemy can trip you up when you rely fully on the Hand that is able to keep you from stumbling! Truth number 2 is found in John 10:28 (NIV) *I give them eternal life, and they shall never perish; no one will snatch them out of my hand.* Remembering Who our God is helps us to weather the schemes of the enemy, undaunted.

- Psalm 141 encourages me to remember Who my Source of strength is. In the NLT verses 4, 5, 8 and 9 reveal that the psalmist is not placing his confidence in himself but rather in God. Paraphrasing… don't let me drift toward evil… don't let me refuse godly counsel… I look to You Lord for help… Keep me from the traps my enemies have set. *Draw near to God and he will come near to you. Wash your hands, you sinners, and purify your hearts, you double-minded. James 4:8 (NIV)* It would appear this psalmist in Psalm 141 is asking for God to make him single-mindedly focused on the things of God and not worldly things. No matter how strong we think we are, we are wise to place God before us in all things. He IS before all things (Colossians 1:17) it's just a matter of if we are obediently following Him in ALL things. *So, if you think you are standing firm, be careful that you don't fall! 1 Corinthians 10:12 (NIV)* We would do well to have the same humble attitude of submission to God's leadership as Moses had in Exodus 33:15 (NIV) *Then Moses said to him, "If your Presence does not go with us, do not send us up from here.*

"Cool Down":

_____

_____

_____

_____

_____

_____

_____

God bless you muchly~

~ DAY 29 ~

Date: _____

Welcome! Thank you for hurdling all distractions that could have kept you from coming today. Hurdling is hard work (if near impossible) so if you are feeling a bit sore I hear the best thing for lactic acid burn is to press forward! So let's keep those spiritual muscles moving and jump right in shall we!?!! *Jabez cried out to the God of Israel, "Oh, that you would bless me and enlarge my territory! Let your hand be with me, and keep me from harm so that I will be free from pain." And God granted his request. 1 Chronicles 4:10 (NIV)* Praise the One who is able!

Warm Up and Worship:

_____

_____

Pray Scripture: *Great is the LORD! He is most worthy of praise! No one can measure his greatness. Psalm 145:3 (NLT)* Please continue in prayer as you prepare your heart and mind to meet with our Healer.

P.R. & P.R.

_____

_____

_____

_____

_____

_____

_____

_____

_____

_____

Daily Devotional Reading: "Service in love done with sincerity and truth, is worship."

So then...

So then, don't be afraid. I will provide for you and your children." And he reassured them and spoke kindly to them. Genesis 50:21 (NIV)

It seems Genesis 50:20 is such a popularly quoted verse, *You intended to harm me, but God intended it for good to accomplish what is now being done, the saving of many lives. (NIV),* and rightly so, as it reminds us all of the much needed "but God..." trump card in our lives! However the verse after that one, verse 21, is just as, if not more astounding! Verse 21 gives evidence to the power of God released within a person willing to fully trust and obey; to hang their hope on Jesus Christ alone and who fully understands that the unconditional love of God found in Jesus is stronger than the worst of themselves! How else could one step forward from those that intended to harm them, into... so then I'll just go ahead and comfort you with kind words and provide for you and your next of kin (as verse 21 indicates)?!!

When we are so entwined, so enraptured with the One who has served us first, loved us first, our acts of love and service become motivated by Him and for Him alone - it's an act of self sacrificial worship. *Through Jesus, therefore, let us continually offer to God a sacrifice of praise - the fruit of lips that openly profess his name. Hebrews 13:15 (NIV)*

Remember, *You did not choose me, but I chose you and appointed you so that you might go and bear fruit- fruit that will last- … John 15:16 (NIV) For by grace you have been saved through faith. And this is not your own doing; it is the gift of God, not a result of works, so that no one can boast. Ephesians 2:8-9 (ESV)*

The only way any of us produce acts of service that reflect the love of Christ, is through His Holy Spirit in us, Jesus flowing through us. *"I am the vine; you are the branches. If you remain in me and I in you, you will bear much fruit; apart from me you can do nothing. John 15:5 (NIV)* He is our Source of life and all worthy things that flow from our life. However none of our acts earn us more of His favor, more of His love. On the cross Jesus said, it is finished (John 19:30). He did all the work needed to secure our salvation because we could not, even if we tried. So any good work produced from our lives is a byproduct of God's amazing grace, His connection with us in a love relationship in such a way that He produces in/through us a display of HIS splendor (Isaiah 61:1-4)!

A love relationship requires our surrender to Him who loved us first (John 3:16). Any love relationship requires trust and our trust in God is demonstrated via obedience to His Word. *John 13:34-35 (NIV) "A new command I give you: Love one another. As I have loved you, so you must love one another. By this everyone will know that you are my disciples, if you love one another."* Why is this love the tell tale sign that we belong to Jesus?

Because the kind of love we are to love with is not naturally human (like displayed in Genesis 50:21), we are to love with the love we have received from Jesus and that love cannot be found in this world.

The way we understand the Father's love will determine how well we are able to serve others in love. 1 John 4:11 (NIV) *Dear friends, since God so loved us, we also ought to love one another.* He SO loved you and me with a love that is STRONGER than the stench of the worst parts of ourselves. WOW! What motivation to reflect this kind of love no matter how it is received by the outside world for the sole reason of showing worshipful gratitude to the One who loved us this way!! *1 John 3:16-18 (NIV) This is how we know what love is: Jesus Christ laid down his life for us. And we ought to lay down our lives for our brothers and sisters. If anyone has material possessions and sees a brother or sister in need but has no pity on them, how can the love of God be in that person? Dear children, let us not love with words or speech but with actions and in truth.*

See also James 2:14-26. For where there is genuine faith there will be genuine deeds because faith produces; not in an effort to earn something it doesn't yet have, but rather to prove what it already possesses - a place in the Vine.

Our obedience does not stem from a need to earn our way to God but rather our obedience proves our trust in a God who already paid the way for us to be with Him. *But God demonstrates his own love for us in this: While we were still sinners, Christ died for us. Romans 5:8 (NIV)*

Dear one, may your trust in Jesus, who is your sure hope of salvation, and the One who loves you unconditionally, be proved through your obedience to His Word. May how we serve others in Christ's love be genuine worship and produce in us the kind of worshipers He seeks. *John 4:24 (NKJV) God is Spirit, and those who worship Him must worship in spirit and truth."*

Serving and loving others like Christ first did for us (and continues to do for us) is not easy. At times we will fall short but if our motivation is a love relationship with our God (that He initiated) and Who we trust loves us unconditionally, and Who has given us a sure hope of a better day yet to come, then we can take hold of an unshatterable joy within even unhappy circumstances and continue to follow through in obedience to His Word; submitting a sacrifice of praise in humble worship because He is so worth it.

~~~

Study in the Psalms: Today we will be reading Psalms 142, 143, 144, 145 and 146.

- Converse with God as you read through each Psalm.
- Pause and reflect on verses that catch your heart's attention.
- Record one verse from each Psalm that holds impact for you.
- Review your list. Is there a theme in the verses you highlighted? Take time and listen for God's voice to your heart.

- My favorite verse from Psalm 142:

  _____

  _____

  _____

- My favorite verse from Psalm 143:

  _____

  _____

  _____

- My favorite verse from Psalm 144:

  _____

  _____

  _____

- My favorite verse from Psalm 145:

  _____

  _____

  _____

- My favorite verse from Psalm 146:

  _____

  _____

  _____

Five points to ponder.

- Psalm 142 is by David from inside a cave, most likely during one of the times he was hiding out from king Saul in pursuit of his life! If you feel like your current season is caving in around you, that you are alone, or that no one knows or sees you, take verse three to heart! Psalm 142:3 (NLT) *When I am overwhelmed, you alone know the way I should turn.* … When we are overwhelmed the One who knit our hearts together, Who has never left our side is the only One that truly can satisfy all we crave in the "cave". Revelation 2:19 (NIV) states, *I know your deeds, your love and faith, your service and perseverance, and that you are now doing more than you did at first.* David had been anointed the next king and yet over a decade went by before he took the throne. All the while the current king Saul, sought his life! David probably went through many doubts as to whether he had heard God correctly?! And yet faith in God includes faith in His timing. The Bible does record catastrophic ripple effects of taking matters into our own human hands as if we knew best! David decides to wait in God and on His timing. What might it look like for you to wait IN God and ON His timing?

- Psalm 143:8 is surely among my favorites however today let's look at verse 10 a bit more closely. This Psalm seems to find David deepening into depression and so his prayer (remarkably) is to be taught God's will! How often when we are depressed or down about something it is our problems that consume us and we pray for guidance but how open are we to allowing God to restructure our lives, our perspectives in a down state of mind? We pray and seek looking for what will bring us up, what will "fix" the issue and maybe the only thing needing fixing is our perspective, our priorities… Is it possible that if we were truly willing to be taught by God that what we would learn would transform our "pit" into a "paradise" because of how well it reflects His faithfulness?! If we would truly allow God to awaken our minds I believe it just might stir our will! *Romans 12:2 (NIV) Do not conform to the pattern of this world, but be transformed by the renewing of your mind. Then you will be able to test and approve what God's will is - his good, pleasing and perfect will.* When your heart is heavy, do what David did and turn to God in prayer. Jesus alone knows the depths of despair a soul can go. Just before He went to the cross the following verse is recorded from the Garden of Gethsemane. *Matthew 26:38 (NIV) Then he said to them, "My soul is overwhelmed with sorrow to the point of death.* ... Jesus too dealt with a troubled heart in prayer. ... *take captive every thought to make it obedient to Christ. 2 Corinthians 10:5 (NIV)*

- Psalm 144 reminds us life is short and to not waste it living for a lesser purpose than God has for us. Only in His will, will we find our "sweet spot". Anything else will only find us leaving sweat spots everywhere as we try to work things out in our own strength! Things that He never intended for us to do! This Psalm ends with the reminder that the joy filled person is the one who has spiritual contentment, meaning they are in their "sweet spot". Check out what I mean by reading Habakkuk 3:17-18 (NIV) *Though the fig tree does not but and there are no grapes on the vines, thought he olive crop fails and the fields produce no food, though there are no sheep in the pen and no cattle in the stalls, yet I will rejoice in the Lord, I will be joyful in God my Savior.* When you know your Savior, Jesus Christ, you can always choose to walk in the available power of the resurrection! Choosing to walk forward in the promises of God that no matter how hard things get, we are not alone (Matthew 28:20), this world is not our home (2 Timothy 4:18) and there is purpose for the path. *Romans 8:28 (NIV) And we know that in all things God works for the good of those who love him, who have been called according to his purpose.*

- Psalm 145 is spoken by someone who has an authentic relationship with the Lord. Verses 18-20 display this close relationship. The Lord is close to the one who calls on Him in truth… He grants the desires of the one who fears Him, He hears them and rescues them… He protects those who love Him. There is a special relationship between one who calls, fears, loves the Lord. God will not forsake His children, He is close, responds and protects them! Someone who has this intimate relationship with God has a heart of worship just because he knows His God is worth-it! This Psalm is a reminder of God's good character, He is faithful and gracious, from just His hand EVERY living thing is provided for! When we are tempted to question God's goodness because of all the evil we see in the world we must remember we were the ones who broke it and when God didn't have to, He came to save us from it. Maybe the better wonder question is why is our God so good?!! *Psalm 144:3 (NLT) O LORD, what are human beings that you should notice them, mere mortals that you should think about them? John 15:13 (NIV) Greater love has no one that this: to lay down one's life for one's friends.*

- Psalm 146 is wonderful to me in that it reminds me of another favorite part of mine in Scripture. Back in Matthew 11 when John the Baptist was put in prison and not for doing anything really wrong he began to doubt. When things around him began to look questionable… like he had lived his whole life preparing the way for Jesus, God Himself, so WHY was John the (good guy) Baptist the one in jail?! John sends his buddies out to find Jesus and ask Him if he had gotten things all wrong!? Was Jesus the Messiah or had he been mistaken? This same John who baptized Jesus and saw the sky rip open and the Holy Sprit decent upon Him and the Father say in an audibly voice that this was His Son of whom He was well pleased (see Matthew 3:13-17)!! And yet, when things were looking confusing and John's life was on the line serious doubts began to creep in!! This Psalm 146 reminds us not to put our trust in humans, not in our own skill and smarts for we have no power to save a soul! Psalm 146:6-9 is what reminds me of our story in Matthew because when John's friends bring his question to Jesus He responds in Matthew 11:4-6 (NIV) … *"Go back and report to John what you hear and see: The blind receive sight, the lame walk, those who have leprosy are cleansed, the deaf hear, the dead are raised, and the good news is proclaimed to the poor. Blessed is anyone who does not stumble on account of me."* Dear one, blessed are we who do not become offended by the way He chooses to do things because He knows things we don't and understands things we can't. Psalm 146 begins and ends with "Praise the LORD" reminding us to have a spirit of praise throughout our days, sunrise to sunset because He is faithful and always, always praise worthy! *Revelation 22:13 (NIV) I am the Alpha and the Omega, the First and the Last, the Beginning and the End.*

"Cool Down": What has made you glad you pushed through and studied here today, rather than give in to the distractions of life?

_____

_____

_____

_____

_____

_____

_____

God bless you muchly~

~ DAY 30 ~

Date: _____

Hello my dear friend. I'm glad you are here. Even if I cannot physically see you I'm grateful for the blessing of your presumed presence on the same page as I. Speaking of physical sight, mine falls far short of 20/20. Recently I went for a routine eye exam and like always they show me the big giant 'E' first (I appreciate their hopefulness). However without any eyewear this giant "E" only looks like a grayish cloud. The doctor then proceeds to flip down lens after lens asking if power 1 or 2 is better, 3 or power 4… I find myself inside my head screaming, "MORE POWER, JUST GIVE ME MORE POWER!!" Everything is just out of focus otherwise! This led to a bit of a chuckle.. the kind that just sort of embarrassingly escapes, produced from a random funny thought inside your own head. Leaving everyone around to look at you like your bird has flown the coo-coo's nest for sure (maybe people just look at me like that). Anyway… My experience in the eye doctors office made me think of how often in life we too want to scream, "MORE POWER!", when really in Christ we already have all the power we need we just fail to access it. It's like me failing to put on my glasses in the morning. I have what I need but if I fail to take it up I'm left to feel powerless.

Today dear one, I pray that you and I pay attention to the places in God's Word that He gives us control. Like… *John 14:27 (NIV) Peace I leave with you; my peace I gave you. I do not give to you as the world gives. Do not let your hearts be troubled and do not be afraid.* "Do not let..." He has given us the peace we need to keep calm. We can now choose to exercise the power He has given us to take up that peace and tame the trouble that would threaten our heart. Now get a load of this! In nearly the same address, Matthew 14:27 (we just looked at JOHN 14:27) (Gotta love when God makes it easy to commit His Word to memory!) (NIV) *But Jesus immediately said to them: "Take courage! It is I. Don't be afraid."* See that part where God gave us control? TAKE courage! He has made courage available just as He has His peace, but we must exercise the control He has given us and take up the power He has made available to us. Praise Him for never leaving us stranded, more power is always available to us in Him dear one.

Warm Up and Worship:

_____

_____

Pray Scripture: *All Scripture is God-breathed and is useful for teaching, rebuking and correcting and training in righteousness, so that the servant of God may be thoroughly equipped for every good work. 2 Timothy 3:16-17 (NIV)* Please continue in prayer as you prepare your heart and mind to meet with our Guide.

P.R. & P.R.

_____

_____

_____

_____

_____

_____

_____

_____

_____

_____

Daily Devotional Reading: "Treasure In Your Sack"

"It's all right," he said, "Don't be afraid. Your God, the God of your father, has given you treasure in your sacks;... Genesis 43:23 (NIV)

I find there is an interesting similarity between…

Genesis 43:14 (NIV) …_as for me, if I am bereaved, I am bereaved."_

and…

Esther 4:16 (NIV) …_and if I perish, I perish."_

Both Jacob and Esther were faced with a crossroads of sorts and both had come to the conclusion as Helen Keller would put it… "Life is either a daring adventure or nothing at all." Maybe you too have found that in life we can't always choose the music life plays, but we can choose how we dance to it. Dear one, are you choosing to dance?

Further in Genesis 43 we find Jacob's sons begging for a pardon (verse 20) from a fiasco they caused and yet kinda they didn't (Life can be tricky like that sometimes, can't it?!!). However they approach their predicament from a humble standpoint. *Humble yourselves, therefore, under God's mighty hand, that he may lift you up in due time. 1 Peter 5:6 (NIV)*

The boys are trying to make things right, actually going above and beyond to turn things around and yet they don't know what the outcome will be. *Commit to the LORD whatever you do, and he will establish your plans. Proverbs 16:3 (NIV)*

To their surprise the man in charge responds with, *"It's all right,"* … *"Don't be afraid. … Your God… has given you treasure in your sacks;*…(Gen. 43:23 NIV) Dear one, in Jesus, no matter how many crossroads you may have faced and found yourself to have taken the wrong way - Jesus remains to be the Way back (John 14:6)! It's all right, don't be afraid to repent and turn around as He waits to receive you, wash you with His grace, mercy, forgiveness and unfailing love (2 Peter 3:9-10). *Create in me a pure heart, O God, and renew a steadfast spirit within me. Do not cast me from your presence or take your Holy Spirit from me. Restore to me the joy of your salvation and grant me a willing spirit, to sustain me. Psalm 51:10-12 (NIV)*

After Jacob's sons were told not to fear over their past they were welcomed in and their feet washed!! John 13 records Jesus washing His disciples feet. A reminder that as we walk through life we will find ourselves in fiascoes from time to time, muddied up from our own sin or other's or just that of this broken world. However we are never without hope in Jesus! *But we have this treasure in jars of clay to show that this all-surpassing power is from God and not from us. 2 Corinthians 4:7 (NIV)*

Jesus is your treasure of love within, and you always gain by giving Love!

By God's amazing grace He continues to transform sinful sacks into treasure troves of His Living Hope! Now that's music we can all dance to! Who can you invite to this dance floor of Living Hope?

~~~

Study in the Psalms: Today we will be reading Psalms 147, 148, 149, 150. *Just four Psalms today and we will circle back around to Psalm 119 to wrap things up tomorrow!

- Converse with God as you read through each Psalm.
- Pause and reflect on verses that catch your heart's attention.
- Record one verse from each Psalm that holds impact for you.
- Review your list. Is there a theme in the verses you highlighted? Take time and listen for God's voice to your heart.

- My favorite verse from Psalm 147:

  _____

  _____

  _____

- My favorite verse from Psalm 148:

  _____

  _____

  _____

- My favorite verse from Psalm 149:

  _____

  _____

  _____

- My favorite verse from Psalm 150:

  _____

  _____

  _____

Four points to ponder.

- Psalm 147:10-11 reminds us that God is not impressed with the things that seem to captivate humans so easily. Verse 11 (NIV) states, _the LORD delights in those who fear him, who put their hope in his unfailing love._ This also reminds me of the instruction found in _1 Peter 5:6 (NIV) Humble yourselves, therefore, under God's mighty hand, that he may life you up in due time._ Dear one, I don't know if you need this reminder as much as I do, but the same hand that is lifting up the humble is the same Almighty palm that hangs each star in the sky and calls each by name (verse 4)!! Not only that but that is the very same Hand that binds up the broken heart!! Talk about powerful placed perfection on a palpitating heart willing to beat for His!! Will we choose to utilize the control He has given us to trust Him, His ways, leaving our timing in His all wise and powerful hand?! We can trust His Word through which all things (even you and I) are powerfully sustained. *The Son is the radiance of God's glory and the exact representation of his being, sustaining all things by his powerful word. After he had provided purification for sins, he sat down at the right hand of the Majesty in heaven. Hebrews 1:3 (NIV)*

• Psalm 148 is a beautiful picture of a world wide choir is it not!!?! ALL creation is to sing His praise! Individually we are to sing and yet as we sing we join in the larger body of believers as a whole. How well are we "singing" our part? It's easy to bow out because we have compared our "voice" to another and decided theirs is better, more effective. It's also easy to drown out because we feel we deserve more screen time, have more experience to share. Glory be the day when we neither bow out or drown out but just sing out for an audience of One! *For just as each of us has one body with many members, and these members do not all have the same function, so in Christ we, though many, form one body, and each member belongs to all the others. Romans 12:4-5 (NIV)* We are all just better, together. *1 Thessalonians 5:11 (NIV) Therefore encourage on another and build each other up, just as in fact you are doing.*

• Psalm 149:1 encourages us to sing to God a NEW song! I see this as encouragement to not let our relationship with our Creator grow stagnant. There is always a new reason to sing His praises every morning! Swim in His Word, find a new verse to memorize and sing it out throughout the day. Pray that He captivate you with His Word and then may you be enraptured by His love that you find within!

- Psalm 150 reminds me that the only people excluded from the command to praise our God are dead people. Verse 6 clearly states, *Let everything that has breath praise the LORD. Praise the LORD.* There are no excuses, if we are breathing we have a reason to praise God and we are to do it. Not only because He is worthy of it but also because (in His infinite grace and love) He knows we too will benefit!! Isaiah 61:3 tells us a spirit of despair is overcome by putting on His offered garment of praise!!! Oh dear one, I praise God for the breath in our lungs that has sustained our meeting that we might put on that "one size fits all" garment of praise and worship our Creator together; for such a time as this!

"Cool Down": What treasured new song has He given you to sing?

_____

_____

_____

_____

_____

_____

_____

God bless you muchly~

~ DAY 31 ~

Date: _____

Hello dear one, this is our last day and "good-bye's" are never my favorite. So we won't linger in it for in Christ there are no "good-bye's" only "see you soon's"! I do want to thank you with all of my heart for joining me. I hope you too felt like we were just two old friends sitting across the table from one another just devouring His Word as He developed within us an insatiable hunger for more!

May you ever be enraptured by His Word and captivated by His unfailing love for you dear one… oh here come the tears!! We better get a move on as we have much to dive into today within the water of His Word and I'm sure you too would like to do so without having to wade through the waterworks of our eyes! Just know you are precious to me as someone God answered my prayers with and for such a time as this, by His amazing grace, our paths have crossed the same page. Thank you muchly dear one. *And this is my prayer: that your love may abound more and more in knowledge and depth of insight, so that you may be able to discern what is best and may be pure and blameless for the day of Christ, filled with the fruit of righteousness that comes through Jesus Christ - to the glory and praise of God. Philippians 1:9-11 (NIV)*

Warm Up and Worship:

_____

_____

Pray Scripture: *Direct my footsteps according to your word; let no sin rule over me. Psalm 119:133 (NIV)* Please continue in prayer as you prepare your heart and mind to meet with our Alpha and Omega, our Beginning and End.

P.R. & P.R.

_____

_____

_____

_____

_____

_____

_____

_____

_____

_____

Daily Devotional Reading: "You Will Make It!"

And God said, "I will be with you. And this will be a sign to you that it is I who have sent you: When you have brought the people out of Egypt, you will worship God on this mountain." Exodus 3:12 (NIV)

"WHEN you... you WILL worship God on this mountain." The verse above is spoken with confidence, with assurance that the trial will be overcome, you will make it to the mountain top! You will make it and not just barely but with energy to worship! So dear one, don't give up!! In God's strength you can make it out of "Egypt" to the mountain top… worshiping (Philippians 4:13)!

It was in Genesis 13:11 that Lot and Abraham parted ways (which was the beginning of Lot's downfall). Abraham and Lot were parting to keep the peace. At first it sounds like a good idea right?! How easy is it to come up with excuses to give up, to part ways with a job, an activity, a relationship… you name it. When looking for an excuse to give up or give in, we are all sure to find one along with probably some pretty good validating points (just like Abraham and Lot)!

Instead of parting to "keep the peace" have we first tried inviting the Prince of Peace (Isaiah 9:6) to our equation? *For he himself is our peace, who has made the two groups one and has destroyed the barrier, the dividing wall of hostility, Ephesians 2:14 (NIV). Therefore what God has joined together, let no one separate." Mark 10:9 (NIV)*

Even if, even when we have fallen short and done things our own way only to find ourselves rolling downhill, we have a God who can redeem, restore, make strong, firm and steadfast again (1 Peter 5:10) by His amazing grace! Back in Exodus the Israelites journey was not perfect and yet they made it just as God had said! Even though Lot's life took a turn downhill it was through one of his biggest debacles that Ruth, a Moabite, became the great grandmother of David through whose line our Messiah came! Praise our Redeemer!

Our God shows no favoritism (Romans 2:11) and God sustains and protects His own. Through faith and belief in Jesus Christ as our Savior (John 3:16) we become His child and ALL God's children

(Galatians 3:26) make it to the mountain top! He won't give up on you, don't give up on Him. *But when you ask, you must believe and not doubt, because the one who doubts is like a wave of the sea, blown and tossed by the wind. James 1:6 (NIV) ... If you do not stand firm in your faith, you will not stand at all." Isaiah 7:9 (NIV)*

Keep on dear one, you will make it, the mountain top is coming so join me in worshiping our Warrior King; the One who has won! *"And I, because of what they have planned and done, am about to come and gather the people of all nations and languages, and they will come and see my glory. "I will set a sign among them, and I will send some of those who survive to the nations- to Tarshish, to the Libyans and Lydians (famous for archers), to Tubal and Greece, and to the distant islands that have not heard of my fame or seen my glory. They will proclaim my glory among the nations. And they will bring all your people, from all the nations, to my holy mountain... Isaiah 66:18-20 (NIV)*

~~~

Study of Psalm 119:

Psalm 119 is not only the longest Psalm but also the longest chapter in the Bible. This Psalm is broken up into 22 parts. Each part is headed by a Hebrew letter of the Alphabet AND each verse within each segment begins with that letter! So... just a simple study tip in case you were planning on memorizing Psalm 119, it would probably be easiest in Hebrew. (I guess in my case, I'd have to learn fluent Hebrew first!!) Another interesting thing about this Psalm is that almost every verse mentions God's Word! The longest book in the

Bible is centered on the value and importance of it!! One challenge would be to take a pencil and circle every time in Psalm 119 God's Word is referenced either with the word, "Word" or "law" or "precepts" or any word that makes reference to His Word. Just to visually see how intentional this Psalm is on focusing our attention on what is really important. We can look the world over, and pay exorbitant amounts of money for counseling when His Word will always be our best counsel, holding all the answers we need for doing life well! His Word is living and active but it is only with the help of the Holy Spirit that we can read it with the understanding and application that we should. This is why prayer before reading is so important. The words are just black and white ink on a page unless the Holy Spirt reads me as I read Him, interpreting for me what I could never understand on my own, teaching me great and unsearchable things I do not know and by His grace helping me to apply it, affecting authentic life change.

Today you will be able to record one verse per Hebrew alphabet grouping. Enjoy!

- Converse with God as you read through each grouping.
- Pause and reflect on verses that catch your heart's attention.
- Record one verse from each group that holds impact for you.
- Review your list. Is there a theme in the verses you highlighted? Take time and listen for God's voice to your heart.

- Aleph - Your favorite verse between 1-8.

  _____

  _____

- Beth - Your favorite verse between 9-16.

  _____

  _____

- Gimel - Your favorite verse between 17-24.

  _____

  _____

- Daleth - Your favorite verse between 25-32.

  _____

  _____

- He - Your favorite verse between 33-40.

  _____

  _____

- Waw - Your favorite verse between 41-48.

  _____

  _____

- Zayin - Your favorite verse between 49-56.

  _____

  _____

- Heth - Your favorite verse between 57-64.

  _____

  _____

- Teth - Your favorite verse between 65-72.

  _____

  _____

- Yodh - Your favorite verse between 73-80.

  _____

  _____

- Kaph - Your favorite verse between 81-88.

  _____

  _____

- Lamedh - Your favorite verse between 89-96.

  _____

  _____

- Mem - Your favorite verse between 97-104.

  _____

  _____

  _____

- Nun - Your favorite verse between 105-112.

  _____

  _____

  _____

- Samekh - Your favorite verse between 113-120.

  _____

  _____

  _____

- Aylin - Your favorite verse between 121-128.

  _____

  _____

  _____

- Pe - Your favorite verse between 129-136.

  _____

  _____

  _____

- Tsadhe - Your favorite verse between 137-144.

  _____

  _____

  _____

- Qoph - Your favorite verse between 145-152.

  _____

  _____

  _____

- Resh - Your favorite verse between 153-160.

  _____

  _____

  _____

- Sin and Shin - Your favorite verse between 161-168.

  _____

  _____

  _____

- Taw - Your favorite verse between 169-176.

  _____

  _____

  _____

Today's bullet points will look a bit different so let's just take it one letter at a time, shall we?!

- **Aleph** (verses 1-8) God's Word is our best way and is to be fully obeyed. This psalmist wisely acknowledges this and his need for God's help. The Bible is the only rule book in which the Author promises to come along side us and sustain us, support us every step of the way. He is faithful. Will we choose to be, to take Him at His Word, to follow in humble obedience as He faithfully leads? _Psalm 32:8 (NIV) I will instruct you and teach you in the way you should go;_

I will counsel you with my loving eye on you. Hebrews 13:5 (NIV) Keep your lives free from the love of money and be content with what you have, because God has said, "Never will I leave you; never will I forsake you."

- **Beth** (verses 9-16) This world is contaminated with sin, so how are we, as people living emerged in such an environment to keep pure?! God's Word. Verse 11 encourages us to memorize it, hide it in our hearts where it can never be lost, an ever present help and guide!

- **Gimel** (verses 17-24) God gives rules to afford us the abundant life He died to give us and to save us from our own destruction! Verse 21 reminds us it's those who stray from the Way that end up cursed. We have all been given the same warning, so I pray verse 18 (NIV). *Open my eyes that I may see wonderful things in our law.* His Way is The wonderful Way, help me Lord to desire it as such and not let the things of this world and my own sinful desires drag me away (James 1:14).

- **Daleth** (verses 25-32) The psalmist is weary but has set his heart on where he knows true refreshment for a weary soul will come from (verse 28). *Then, because so many people were coming and going that they did not even have a chance to eat, he said to them, "Come with me by yourselves to a quiet place and get some rest." Mark 6:31 (NIV)*

- **He** (verses 33-40) The psalmist knows where true happiness is found. He is asking for help to fix his eyes there because this world can be loud and distracting. *Colossians 3:1-2 (NIV) Since, then, you have been raised with Christ, set your hearts on things above, where Christ is, seated at the right hand of God. Set your minds on things above, not on earthly things.* (See also Philippians 4:8) That speaks of setting our mind and heart on things above which sounds like a total focus. Why? Because that is where our enduing strength to run well our race and escape the corruption of this world lies! *Therefore, since we are surrounded by such great cloud of witnesses, let us throw off everything that hinders and the sin that so easily entangles. Let us run with perseverance the race marked out for us, fixing our eyes on Jesus, the pioneer and perfecter of faith. For the joy set before him he endured the cross, scorning its shame, and sat down at the right hand of the throne of God. Consider him who endured such opposition from sinners, so that you will not grow weary and lose heart. Hebrews 12:1-3 (NIV)*

- **Waw** (verses 41-48) Only in Christ do we truly walk in freedom (verse 45). Free from the chains of sin and regret, free to move forward in faith! *If we confess our sins, he is faithful and just and will forgive us our sins and purify us from all unrighteousness. 1 John 1:9 (NIV) Therefore, if anyone is in Christ, the new creation has come: The old has gone, the new is here! 2 Corinthians 5:17 (NIV)*

- **Zayin** (verses 49-56) This section begins with "remember..". Praise God we have been given an Advocate to help us remember when we have forgotten (see John 14:26) however if we have not spent time pouring into our spiritual bank at the time we need to make a withdraw we might be sorely disappointed! Time in His Word in season and out is imperative to our mental and physical well being! Verse 50 (NIV) *My comfort in my suffering is this: Your promise preserves my life.* Dear one, God has given us great and precious promises to bank on but do we know them? For believers in Jesus this world is the worst it will ever get. For those who do not believe in Jesus this world is the best is will ever be and how sad to live in such hopelessness when such Living Hope is available!!

- **Heth** (verses 57-64) Verse 62 correlates to verse 55 from our last section for me. In the night when we cannot sleep, He is there and instead of defaulting to worry we can worship. Get up and give thanks that even still, *The light shines in the darkness, and the darkness has not overcome it. John 1:5 (NIV)* What Scriptural promise holds a prominent place in your mind to steady your heart in the dark?

- **Teth** (verses 65-72) This section reminds me of the many times in the Bible we are reminded that God disciplines those He loves. See Hebrews 12:3-11, Psalm 94:12, John 15:2 and Proverbs 3:11-12. *Teach me knowledge and good judgment, for I trust your commands, Psalm 119:65 (NIV)* Why oh why do I have to be so stubborn and learn things the hard way?! Jesus was perfect start to finish and He still was able to gain through His sufferings! See Isaiah 53:11-12 and Hebrews 5:8. We as humans can get better or bitter over our sufferings for whatever reason they are occurring. Maybe the "why" they are occurring isn't as important as to "what" will be produced through it.

- **Yodh** (verses 73-80) Verse 74 stands out to me in that even in the psalmists affliction he desires to be a joy to those who come in contact with him! WOW! That is a heart that has delighted wholeheartedly in the things of God and not self. May verse 80 also be a prayer of my heart, *May I wholeheartedly follow your decrees,* ...

- **Kaph** (verses 81-88) Although worn from the wait the psalmist takes heart in the trustworthy promises of God. The wait can cause a war on the will. However we have a God who understands the hard wait. Jesus sacrificed Himself in our place, to pay our debt and now Hebrews 10 says He waits. *But when this priest had offered for all time one sacrifice for sins, he sat down at the right hand of God, and since that time he waits for his enemies to be made a footstool. Hebrews 10:12-13 (NIV)* WOW talk about a hard wait!! And yet in His amazing grace He waits not wanting there to be any enemies!!!! *The Lord is not slow in keeping his promise, as some understand slowness. Instead he is patient with you, not wanting anyone to perish, but everyone to come to repentance. 2 Peter 3:9 (NIV)*

- **Lamedh** (verses 89-96) If God's eternal, perfect and faithful Word had not been the psalmist joy and delight he would have perished in his suffering. How many hospitals are filled today simply because the soul is devoid of unfailing hope?! In Jesus we can experience an unshakable joy that runs deeper than mere happiness which changes with outward circumstances. *Hebrews 6:19 (NIV) We have this hope as an anchor for the soul, firm and secure. … Nehemiah 8:10 (NIV) … Do not grieve, for the joy of the Lord is your strength." John 16:33 (NIV) "I have told you these things, so that in me you may have peace. In this world you will have trouble. But take heart! I have overcome the world."*

- **Mem** (verses 97-104) This section, especially verse 102, reminds me of a few other places in Scripture that echo this same idea that God is our best teacher. *Isaiah 54:13 (NIV) All your children will be taught by the LORD, and great will be their peace. John 6:45 (NIV) It is written in the Prophets: 'They will all be taught by God.' Everyone who has heard the Father and learned from him comes to me. Acts 4:13 (NIV) When* *they saw the courage of Peter and John and realized that they were unschooled, ordinary men, they were astonished and they took note that these men had been with Jesus.*

- **Nun** (verses 105-112) Goodness we really could have made an entire study out of just Psalm 119! We could spend a whole days devotional on each of these 22 sections but alas we are only able to skim the surface in each of these bullet points. Trusting that the Holy Spirit will bring to light the point He needs each individual heart to receive as only He could perceive. Between verse 107 and 108 I read this psalmist has suffered much and yet is offering willing praise. What could defeat the enemy faster or delight the Father's heart quicker than a sacrifice of praise even if, even when, even though… ?! *Through Jesus, therefore, let us continually offer to God a sacrifice of praise - the fruit of lips that openly profess his name. Hebrews 13:15 (NIV)*

- **Samekh** (verses 113-120) Verse 118 reminds us that straying from God's way never ends well. No matter what illusion of control we grasp at it will only be just that, an illusion. We can stop grasping and start resting in the One who has control and has said that all authority has been given to Him (Matthew 28:18)! How much energy would we conserve if we just took up a single mind and served God with an undivided heart?! All this duplicity, trying to appease people and God is exhausting! People can never be pleased and evil's appetite is never appeased! *"No one can serve two masters. Either you will hate the one and love the other, or you will be devoted to the one and despise the other. You cannot serve both God and money. Matthew 6:24 (NIV) But if serving the LORD seems undesirable to you,* *then choose for yourselves this day whom you will serve, whether the gods your ancestors served beyond the Euphrates, or the gods of the Amorites, in whose land you are living. But as for me and my household, we will serve the LORD." Joshua 24:15 (NIV)*

- **Ayin** (verses 121-128) Verse 125 cry for discernment. Discernment coupled with a desire to apply it equals life change! What good is mosquito bite medicine if I don't apply it to the bite?! I can have the cure and yet still suffer uncured unless I apply the antidote to the place of need! Discernment of God's Word helps us know how to apply it to specific areas of our life but we still need to desire to do so. *Restore to me the joy of your salvation and grant me a willing spirit, to sustain me. Psalm 51:12 (NIV)*

- **Pe** (verses 129-136) It is God's Word that gives light and directs our steps so why do we run to other things? We put our faith in "things" instead of placing it in the One that holds all "things" together (See Colossians 1:17)! May we be given more grace to rely more fully on Him. *""The Lord bless you and keep you; the Lord make his face shine on you and be gracious to you; the Lord turn his face toward you and give you peace."" Numbers 6:24-26 (NIV)*

- **Tsadhe** (verses 137-144) God's Word holds up a contrast to the way of the world. Verse 143 finds the psalmist in trouble and distress and yet it was God's commands that brought delight. Psalm 94:19 (NIV) echos that thought, *When anxiety was great within me, your consolation brought me joy. Romans 12:2 (NIV) Do not conform to the pattern of this world, but be transformed but the renewing of your mind. Then you will be able to test and prove what God's will is - his good, pleasing and perfect will.*

- **Qoph** (verses 145-152) The next time you can't sleep may verse 148 (NIV) be your reason too (or at least become your reason), *My eyes stay open through the watches of the night, that I may meditate on your promises.* Remember, *You will keep in perfect peace those whose minds are steadfast, because they trust in you. Isaiah 26:3 (NIV)*

- **Resh** (verses 153-160) This section states three times in my NIV "preserve my life". The psalmist seems to be fighting for life and banking on the eternal Word and God's character for it. *John 3:16 (NIV) For God so loved the world that he gave his one and only Son, that whoever believes in him shall not perish but have eternal life.* Our God is Living Hope, the tomb still stands empty! We may at times feel like we are fighting for life and yet in reality Life has already fought and won for us!! *Therefore we do not lose heart. Though outwardly we are wasting away, yet inwardly we are being renewed day by day. 2 Corinthians 4:16 (NIV)*

- **Sin and Shin** (verses 161-168) The way this psalmist is able to see beyond his troubles and revel in complete praise all day is a testament to the faithfulness, trustworthiness and effectiveness of God's Word! He is our peace and the lifter of our head to a better perspective, His eternal perspective! *Psalm 3:3 (NIV) But you, LORD, are a shield around me, my glory, the One who lifts my head high. Psalm 119:165 (NIV) Great peace have those who love your law, and nothing can make them stumble.*

- **Taw** (verses 169-176) Interesting when you compare the first verse of Psalm 119 to the last. The psalmist knows God's way is best and yet still struggles with his humans to walk in it. However he honestly and humbly admits his need for a shepherd, The

Shepherd. *I have strayed like a lost sheep. Seek your servant, for I have not forgotten your commands. Psalm 119:176 (NIV)* Dear one, if we are honest we are all like lost sheep without a shepherd but with a shepherd, The Shepherd, everything can change! *For the Son of Man came to seek and to save the lost." Luke 19:10 (NIV) We all, like sheep, have gone astray, each of us has turned to our own way; and the LORD has laid on him the iniquity of us all. Isaiah 53:6 (NIV)* He knew what we were and He came anyway. Love came down that we might live! *Isaiah 53:12 (NLT) I will give him the honors of a victorious soldier, because he exposed himself to death. He was counted among the rebels. He bore the sins of many and interceded for rebels.* "Rebels" does not define the accidental sinner but rather the one who knew better and did wrong anyway. He came for that one too; He died for that one too. He interceded for you, and me too. He wants us all to be with Him in His eternal Kingdom but He will honor our choice. Dear one, may you be enraptured by His Word and captivated by His love for you, eternally.

"Cool Down": Well done my friend! Well done! Today take as much time as you need to go back over the past 31 days. Reflect on the way God has moved in your prayer life and through His Word with you. Record anything God writes on your heart.

_____

_____

_____

_____

_____

_____

_____

_____

_____

_____

_____

_____

_____

_____

_____

_____

_____

_____

_____

_____

_____

I pray that through this study of His Word you have allowed God to romance you into a deeper love relationship with Him, your Creator, your Deliverer, your Defender, your Sustainer, your Strength, your Shield and the Lover of your soul. I pray you have allowed Him to enrapture you with His Word, captivating you with His love dear one!

Thank you most sincerely for allowing me to run my race along side you for such a time as this. Keep running dear one! Run in such a way to pass the baton of faith to the next generations! May God bless you muchly along your journey Home and by His grace may we each be able to declare in confidence, *I have fought the good fight, I have finished the race, I have kept the faith. 2 Timothy 4:7 (NIV)* See you soon!

~Love in Christ, your "running" buddy,
Janette

To him who is able to keep you from stumbling and to present you before his glorious presence without fault and with great joy- to the only God our Savior be glory, majesty, power and authority, through Jesus Christ our Lord, before all ages, now and forevermore! Amen. Jude 24-25 (NIV)

ABOUT: Redeeming grace 99|1 Ministries

Redeeming Grace 99|1 Ministries is based on Matthew 18:12-14. There is no situation, circumstance or life God cannot reach, restore, revive and fully redeem for our good and His glory. Redeeming grace is the criminal on the cross entering into Paradise; it's Ruth the pagan becoming part of Jesus' genealogy; it's Jairus' daughter brought back to life; it's Joseph pulled from the prison and made a mighty leader; it's Daniel on the other side of the lion's den; it's Saul turned Paul; it's Jonah out of the whale; it's David and Bathsheba's son Solomon; it's Hannah having Samuel after barrenness; it's the man lame for 38 years made to walk; it's five loaves and two fish becoming a meal feeding 5,000 with leftovers; it's Lazarus walking out of the tomb; it's the widow's oil that never ran out; it's the parting of the Red Sea and the receding of the Jordan; it's you and I realizing our need for a Savior as we look to Jesus high and lifted up, believing His death on the cross was in our place for our sin, then resurrecting from the grave God defeating the enemy of our souls once and for all. We are made new in receiving the transforming Truth of His love so that we might be made a vessel of His victory. His redeeming grace writes living hope on every page of our lives. You have never laid eyes on someone God did not love. Our mission is to reach one, and then another and another...with the Good News of His redeeming grace for us all through Jesus, raising the population of heaven by His grace, to His glory and praise.

Redeeming Grace 99|1 Ministries
graphic designs © 2020 Design credit: Noah Kieffer
Head shot photo credit: light-and-lens.com

ABOUT THE AUTHOR

By God's amazing grace, Janette resides in Colorado with her husband (married in 2003) their six children and lovable dog named Brave. As a teacher by trade, she finds joy in learning and sharing her passion for the hope filled Word of God. Find other books by Janette Kieffer on Amazon such as...

"Reigning in the Rain" (Volume 1) Walk in the Light of His faithful promises through this one-year journal devotional. When the "rain" in life threatens to flood your heart, remember Who reigns above it all; above the depression, oppression, tragedy, fear, illness, failure, trial, worry, setbacks... Remember the One whose love for you does not change like shifting shadows but remains steadfast and sure. He is Faithful and True, as unshakable today as He was yesterday and will be forever. Remember Whose promises never fail, for our God reigns in, through, and over it all; working (present tense) all things together for our good and His glory. Allow Him to be your understanding in all you do not understand for He says; *When you pass through the waters, I will be with you; and when you pass through the rivers, they will not sweep over you. When you walk through the fire, you will not be burned; the flames will not set you ablaze.* Isaiah 43:2 (NIV) This year, drop your anchor of trust into His faithful promises. For, ...*I know whom I have believed, and am convinced that he is able to guard what I have entrusted to him until that day.* 2 Timothy 1:12 (NIV) He is the Beginning and the End.

"Living Hope" (Volume 2) In this second volume, of one-year Bible study devotional journals, you will dive deeply into the water of His Word and discover there is Living Hope within every storm. With each wave of doubt that threatens to capsize your vessel you have an anchor for your soul firm and secure to which you can cling. Psalm 63:8 (ESV) *My soul clings to you; your right hand upholds me.*

Inside each volume of the journal devotionals you will find 52 weeks of devotionals coupled with weekly extension Scriptures, questions and daily Bible verses to encourage and track your spiritual growth throughout your year. Space to journal your personal reflections and responses is given to provide you with a record at years end of your faith journey and growth in Jesus. The hope is that this Bible study journal will afford you a clearer perspective of our God, painting for you a beautiful picture of His faithful presence with you always. *The LORD is my light and my salvation; whom shall I fear? The LORD is the stronghold of my life; of whom shall I be afraid?* Psalm 27:1 (ESV)

"Everlasting Joy" (Volume 3) In this third volume in the one-year Bible devotional journals, by Janette Kieffer. Come discover how everlasting joy is experienced; walking in the resurrection power of the Champion of heaven! *And because of his glory and excellence, he has given us great and precious promises. These are the promises that enable you to share his divine nature and escape the world's corruption caused by human desires.* 2 Peter 1:4 (NLT) My prayer is that we learn together to live as a joy filled vessel of His victory. *...for the joy of the Lord is your strength."* Nehemiah 8:10 (NIV)

"TRUST in The Light" is book one in a 4 part series called L.I.G.H.T. (Life In God Holds Truth). This series studies the life of Jesus through the harmony of the four gospels. Go back to what you know to find your faith in all that you do not. Allow God to use your questions, doubts, fears, failures, even your triumphs as tools to bring Truth into the Light. Truth you never would have known otherwise. With the rock of ever-increasing TRUST lay the first steppingstone of your faith on the firm foundation of the Faithful and True. He is the same yesterday, today and forever. In an ever-changing world come delight yourself in the Light of God's love for you that will not falter, fail or fade. TRUST in the Light.

"LIVE in The Light" is book two in the L.I.G.H.T. series. This 10 week study book takes us further into the life of Jesus. Upon the solid foundation of Christ we place our trust that we may truly step into life as He intended it to be lived. In a world with ever fluctuating standards of validation, come delight yourself in Him who remains unchanging and steadfast throughout he ages. Through His life we learn to live with great expectancy rather than tangled and tripped up in our faulty expectations. Come step into the Light of His lavish love for you and LIVE!

"REST in The Light" Who understands insanely busy and intense life pressures more than Jesus?! Our God sweat drops of blood in the Garden of Gethsemane in prayer over the severe burden He was enduring on our behalf! Yet at the end of that prayer as the enemy approached Jesus stood and said, "Arise, let's go." not, "Arise let's panic and run!". Our God victoriously faced head on the rush of this world resting in The Father. In this part three of the L.I.G.H.T. series we will embark through another 10 weeks of study diving ever deeper into the life of Christ through the harmony of the four gospels (Matthew, Mark, Luke and John). In a world that spins on busy and runs on filtered picture-perfect displays of altered reality, come rest your heart in the nail scarred palm of the true Prince of Peace. REST in God and let Him build His authentic purpose through you. God only builds beautiful things that display His splendor. A seed in the soil just rests, it rests even when it's dark, cold and dirty; it remains still, trusting the process…They are the shoot I have planted, the work of my hands, for the display of my splendor. Isaiah 60:21 (NIV) God builds, God plants, God works, and by His amazing grace God will make us a display of His splendor if only we will stay RESTING in His mighty capable and trustworthy hands. REST, trust His process and grow to truly live in His victory! …"Come with me by yourselves to a quiet place and get some rest." ~Jesus (Mark 6:31 NIV)

"VICTORY in The Light" Through this fourth and final book in the L.I.G.H.T. series we will walk through the last days of Jesus' life on earth. We will dance through the harmony of the four gospels in order to gain clearer spiritual vision in all that we cannot yet physically see. Though finding all the answers can fill our mind with knowledge, our hearts can still be left void of significance, love, hope, healing… the things our souls truly long for. Within this 10 week in-depth Bible study we will be seeking an authentic encounter with our Savior, Jesus Christ. We will go back to what we know (our stones of remembrance, so to speak) to find our faith in all that we do not. Our Savior lives and reigns victorious! So come fill up your heart with all the fullness of Him. It is in trusting in His faithfulness that we become a vessel of His victory. In Him our end is just the beginning! Jude 1:25 (NLT) All glory to him who alone is God, our Savior through Jesus Christ our Lord. All glory, majesty, power, and authority are his before all time, and in the present, and beyond all time! Amen.

"For Such A Time As This" What does it look like to do life in the power of the resurrection? How do you trust the wit and wisdom of God beyond what you can see and feel? Dear one, it's when our physical sight feels blind, that our spiritual vision has a chance to grow! Allowing the Holy Spirit to fill us, cultivates a heart of perseverance that thrives in His strength. May our Champion of Heaven enrapture our souls through an in-depth study of His Truthful Word. Let no trial or challenge temper the joy found in knowing you were made to be a vessel of His victory… for such a time as this!

"S.O.L.E" (Serve Other's in Christ's Love, Everywhere) Through this four week Bible study I pray you will be encouraged to use the ground beneath your own two soles to live out the Truth in your soul. …"'Love the Lord your God with all your heart and with all your soul and with all your strength and with all your mind'; and, 'Love your neighbor as yourself.'" Luke 10:27 (NIV) By this everyone will know that you are my disciples, if you love one another."

John 13:35 (NIV) You have been given a sphere of influence and The Author of all time and space doesn't waste it. Our great God Almighty, our Choreographer of this dance called life, has called you to the stage. You have been given the leading role in your own life, but only in dancing out His choreography, His way, in His timing will we find fulfillment. As you embark on this study I pray it's His music that delights your soul and sends your sole's dancing into this world with strength, joy, hope, love and peace that cannot be contained but must be shared dear one. Let's dance!

Made in the USA
Las Vegas, NV
25 February 2022